STUDIES IN ECONOMICS AND POLITICAL SCIENCE

Volume 4

THE DISTRIBUTION OF THE PRODUCT

T0271124

THE DISTRIBUTION OF THE PRODUCT

JOHN CRAVEN

Routledge
Taylor & Francis Group

LONDON AND NEW YORK

First published in 1979 by George Allen & Unwin Ltd

This edition first published in 2022
by Routledge

4 Park Square, Milton Park, Abingdon, Oxon OX14 4RN

and by Routledge
605 Third Avenue, New York, NY 10017

Routledge is an imprint of the Taylor & Francis Group, an informa business

Copyright © 1979 by Taylor & Francis.

British Library Cataloguing in Publication Data
A catalogue record for this book is available from the British Library

ISBN: 978-1-03-212459-9 (Set)
ISBN: 978-1-00-322951-3 (Set) (ebk)
ISBN: 978-1-03-212471-1 (Volume 4) (hbk)
ISBN: 978-1-03-212620-3 (Volume 4) (pbk)
ISBN: 978-1-00-322472-3 (Volume 4) (ebk)

DOI: 10.4324/9781003224723

Publisher's Note
The publisher has gone to great lengths to ensure the quality of this reprint but points out that some imperfections in the original copies may be apparent.

Disclaimer
The publisher has made every effort to trace copyright holders and would welcome correspondence from those they have been unable to trace.

The Distribution of the Product

JOHN CRAVEN

Senior Lecturer in Economics,
University of Kent at Canterbury

London
GEORGE ALLEN & UNWIN
Boston   Sydney

First published in 1979

GEORGE ALLEN & UNWIN LTD
40 Museum Street, London WC1A 1LU

© George Allen & Unwin (Publishers) Ltd, 1979

British Library Cataloguing in Publication Data

Craven, John
  The distribution of the product.
  – (Studies in economics; 16).
  1. Income distribution
  2. National income
  I. Title   II. Series
  339.2'01   HB601   79–40001

  ISBN 0–04–339014–5
  ISBN 0–04–339015–3 Pbk

Typeset in 10 on 11 point Times by George Over Limited, London and Rugby
and printed in Great Britain
by William Clowes, Beccles and London

PREFACE

The purpose of this book is to introduce a theory of the distribution of national income between wages, profits and other categories of income. The relation between this branch of distribution theory and other areas of economics is explained in the Introduction.

The first six chapters are designed to introduce distribution theory to students of intermediate economic principles. The prerequisites are found in elementary economics courses; the reader should be familiar with the basic analysis of supply, demand and market equilibrium, and with the use of indifference curves to represent a consumer's preferences. From macroeconomics we shall make use of the national income accounts and the equality of national income, national product and national expenditure in the circular flow of income. Certain basic ideas on the maintenance of full employment are used in Chapter 6, but very little in the way of Keynesian theory is introduced before Chapter 10.

The remaining seven chapters discuss developments of the theory introduced in the first six. Chapters 7–10 can be tackled in any order; students of intermediate economics may find Chapters 8 and 10 somewhat easier to digest than Chapters 7 and 9. Chapters 11–13 must be read in sequence; Chapter 13 is more suited to those who wish to specialise in the study of economic theory.

Many of the important parts of the theory are incorporated in diagrams, and it is essential also that the reader should be able to follow some algebraic manipulation and recognise the formula for a straight line. There is no matrix algebra or set theory, and the only appearance of differential calculus is in an appendix which is not necessary for the development of our main theme. The main mathematical requirement is that the reader should recognise from a formula that one variable depends on another. The exact formula representing this dependency is usually of smaller importance than the dependency itself.

Most of the references to the literature are listed in the notes on the literature at the end of each chapter. Some of the references are to works on which our theory is based, some to complementary texts and some to books and articles that go beyond the theory set out here. Some of the references in this last category require considerably more mathematics than is used in this book. All the references in the text and the notes are referred to by the author's name and a date; the Bibliography contains a complete list.

My own interest in distribution theory and the related areas of capital and growth stems from the teaching of Mario Nuti and Luigi Pasinetti in Cambridge and from a stimulating series of lectures given by Robert Solow of the Massachusetts Institute of Technology. Since coming to teach in Canterbury, I have taught this material to several classes of students, and I have learned much more from their comments and questions. I have had many valuable discussions with Charles Kennedy. Tony Thirlwall, Thea Sinclair and Richard Disney read through an earlier draft, and I am extremely grateful to them for their comments. Roger Vickerman read through the final typescript and rescued me from a variety of errors; those that remain are entirely my own responsibility. Karen Bramley typed drafts and made order out of a chaotic manuscript. My greatest debt is to Laura Craven for all her help and encouragement.

John Craven
Canterbury
August 1978

CONTENTS

THE DISTRIBUTION OF THE PRODUCT

*To my parents
in appreciation*

CHAPTER 1

Introduction

1.1 DISTRIBUTION IN THEORY AND PRACTICE

The study of the distribution of national income has traditionally been divided into several parts. A distinction has grown up in theoretical work between the *functional* distribution and the *personal* distribution. In this book we shall concentrate on the functional distribution between different categories of income, such as *wages*, *profits* and *rents*. This kind of theory divides national income between people who provide different kinds of factors of production, such as labour, capital goods and land. An individual may receive income from several factors of production: a self-employed businessman may own the equipment that he uses and so receive an income that is partly the wages of his labour and partly the profits on his equipment; a worker may accumulate savings, buy shares in a firm and receive an income from these shares, so that his total income is made up of wages and profits. The study of the personal distribution of income examines the incomes of individuals regardless of the factor of production from which the income is derived. Functional distribution theory examines the incomes of suppliers of factors of production regardless of the fact that a particular individual may supply more than one factor.

Attached to each of these areas of theoretical study is a considerable body of empirical literature. It is possible to derive from published national accounts the fact that in the United Kingdom incomes from employment (wages and salaries) are approximately 75 per cent of national income, although there is some evidence that the share of wages and salaries increased towards 80 per cent in 1975 and 1976. The other 25 per cent divides between profits (including interest and dividends) and rent from land and buildings. In the United Kingdom rent has risen from about 4.8 per cent of national income in the mid 1950s to about 7.2 per cent twenty years later. These approximate figures raise certain econometric prob-

1

lems; for example, all the income of the self-employed is included in the share of wages and salaries even though some of their income is profit on the equipment that they own. Also, the measurement of profits in a period of inflation requires a detailed treatment of the gains made by owners of stocks of goods compared with those who hold money or other financial assets. It is not clear that these and other problems of measurement have been adequately dealt with in the published national accounts. International comparisons of the functional distribution involve even greater econometric difficulties, as different countries have different accounting conventions and different ways of presenting the accounts.

Empirical work has also been done on the personal distributions of both income and wealth. In the United Kingdom the Royal Commission on the Distribution of Income and Wealth (HMSO, 1975) is a useful source of information of this kind; it also discusses some of the difficulties of collecting and analysing the necessary data. Other references will be found in the notes on the literature at the end of this chapter.

One of the principal reasons for studying forces determining the distribution of income and for accumulating empirical evidence is the practical question of changing the distribution. For example, the government may feel that the existing personal distribution is unfair and that it can be improved by increasing the share of national income received by wage earners. Functional distribution theory examines the main determinants of the wage earners' share and so indicates to the government how it might try to influence individual behaviour to bring about the desired result. Distribution theory is therefore closely related to welfare economics and to underlying ethical theories that discuss criteria of justice and the problems that arise when governments attempt to take account of the views of individuals in determining their policies. The welfare economics discussed by, for example, Arrow (1951), Graaff (1957), Sen (1970a), Mayston (1974) and Phelps (1973) is therefore highly relevant if distribution theory is used in the formulation of economic policy.

In this book we shall not discuss these related areas. Our task is to examine the forces that determine the division of the national product between the suppliers of labour, capital goods and land. We shall refer to the incomes of those who supply labour as *wages*, even though some refer to their incomes by other names, such as salaries. When we refer to the 'share of wages' we refer to the part of national income that is received by those who supply labour. The income of those who supply land is *rent*; and, subject to certain qualifications and amendments later in the book, the incomes of those who own machinery and equipment and of those who lend money to others to buy machinery and equipment are taken together and referred to as *profit*. This last category plainly includes the incomes that many people refer to as interest or dividends, but these distinctions do not have any great significance for our work. We shall reserve the term *'interest'* for a special purpose in Chapter 5, whilst in Chapter 10 we shall examine the incomes of those who are prepared to take risks. We shall call the income of risk takers *entrepreneurial income*; and, for example, the dividends on shares contain an element of entrepreneurial income as well as an element of profit, since shareholders take the risk that they will lose their money if the company fails. These definitions and the precise framework in which they are used are discussed more fully later in the book.

1.2 DISTRIBUTION THEORY IN MACROECONOMICS AND MICROECONOMICS

MARKETS

Our first task is to show how the theory of the functional distribution of income is related to microeconomic price theory and to macroeconomics. Virtually the first lesson of economic theory is that the price of a good is determined by the forces of supply and demand in a market economy. The supply curve of corn tells us how the quantity of corn that farmers are willing to produce varies with the price that they receive. It also reflects the fact that speculators may release stockpiled corn if the price is high enough. The supply curve reflects the general conditions of production (such as the weather, the rent of farmland, the wages of farm workers, the cost of fertiliser) and of storage (the rent of ware-houses, the cost of fire insurance). The demand curve tells us how much consumers will buy at any price, and so it reflects the incomes of customers, the prices of substitutes for corn, the expectations of speculators (who will buy if they foresee price rises from which they can benefit), and so on. The intersection of the supply curve and the demand curve determines the equilibrium price. The

3

market price of corn affects the farmers who sell it and the standard of living of those who consume it.

We can argue likewise about other goods that people consume and also about those which do not enter directly into the consumers' shopping lists but which, like the farmer's tractors, are used in the production of consumable goods. If the price of tractors rises, the producers of tractors will gain, and the farmer will lose out unless he can pass on the increase in his costs to the consumers by increasing the price of corn. If the farmer can pass on his cost increase, the consumers will lose out as their cost of living rises. The prices of machinery are therefore also instrumental in determining the distribution of real incomes.

Market analysis can be extended to labour also. The labour of plumbers will be demanded by those with leaking pipes and will be supplied by those who have anticipated that the wages of plumbers will be sufficient to make it worth their while to acquire the skills of the trade. Once again the demand and supply curves will determine an equilibrium price, which is the wage of plumbers. These market-determined wages affect the real incomes of those who must pay them: if the wage of tractor mechanics increases, the profits of farmers are likely to fall; if the wage of barbers rises, all but the most unkempt consumers will be somewhat worse off.

So according to elementary economic theory the forces of supply and demand underlie the relative well-being of the individuals in the economy. To examine the functional distribution of income we need to know the wages of various types of labour, the prices of machines and of other inputs to production and the prices of final products. Furthermore, because capitalists buy machines to benefit from their future productivity, and because speculators buy corn or gold to benefit from future price rises, the operation of the market economy requires that individuals have expectations about future price movements. We need to know about demands and supplies in many markets both now and in the future. Our task has grown enormously from the simple analysis of demand and supply in a single market. But worse is yet to come, since the many markets that we must examine are inter-related. The demand curve for corn depends upon barbers' wages; if their wages rise (and if they do not regard corn as an inferior good), they will demand more corn at any given price, so that the demand curve DD in Figure 1 will shift to the right to $D'D'$ and the equilibrium price will change from OP to OP'. A similar shift to the right is likely to occur if rice becomes more expensive, causing people to shift their demand to a cheaper substitute. If tractors become cheaper, farmers may be willing to use more of them and produce more corn, so that the supply curve shifts outwards from *SS* to *S'S'*.

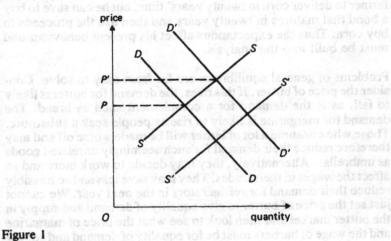

Figure 1

GENERAL EQUILIBRIUM

It is clear that, if we pursue this approach to the question of the distribution of income, the traditional partial-equilibrium analysis, which looks at one market at a time holding all other prices and wages constant, will not be useful. We need to know about many related markets all at once; we have a problem of *general equilibrium*. In these problems the demand and supply of each good can depend not only on its own price but also on the prices of every other good and on the wage of every kind of labour. We have to find a whole set of prices and wages, one for each good and each type of labour, that give equality of demand and supply in every market simultaneously. In so far as current demands and supplies depend on expectations of future prices and wages, these expected prices and wages must be incorporated into the analysis. This can be done in two ways. For some commodities there are *futures markets* established in which it is possible to contract now to buy or sell copper or coffee or Swiss francs, for example, a month or a year ahead. These futures prices reflect expectations about the future availability and desirability of these goods. The second way in which individual expectations are shown is through *savings behaviour*. An individual may save now for his retirement as he expects a lower income when he finishes work. He may also save if he expects that the price of food will rise in relation to his income in order to maintain his standard of living. He cannot now pay a farmer to deliver corn in twenty years' time, but he can save to buy a bond that matures in twenty years and then use the proceeds to buy corn. Thus the expectations affect his present behaviour and must be built into the analysis.

Problems of general equilibrium are far from easy to solve. Consider the price of butter. If this rises, the demand for butter is likely to fall, as is the demand for a complement such as bread. The demand for margarine is likely to rise as people seek a substitute. Those who consume a lot of butter will be made worse off and may therefore reduce their demand for such seemingly unrelated goods as umbrellas. Alternatively, they may decide to work more and so affect the wages in their trades. They may save less and so possibly reduce their demand for refrigerators in the next year. We cannot just set the price of butter to give equality of demand and supply in the butter market and then look to see what the price of margarine and the wage of barbers must be for equality of demand and supply in those markets; for if the barbers' wage is reduced by the extra labour supply of barbers who want to maintain their consumption of butter, the demands for butter and margarine will be affected as some barbers are worse off and some of their customers are better off. We cannot look at one market at a time in our search for a set of prices giving general equilibrium of all demands and supplies; we must consider all prices at once.

General equilibrium theory is an important and complicated branch of economics. It can be shown that there are circumstances in which no equilibrium set of prices (by which we mean a set of prices giving demand equal to supply in all markets simultaneously) can be found, and many interesting theorems have been proved showing that such a set of prices does exist in other circumstances. References to texts in this area can be found in the notes on the literature. Some authors (particularly Bliss, 1975) have concentrated on the intertemporal aspects of general equilibrium by looking at the role of futures markets in distribution theory. Considerable mathematics is needed to follow much of the literature in this area; the simple algebra and geometry that we shall use is rarely enough to demonstrate even the simplest results of general equilibrium analysis involving many goods.

6

A better reason than mathematical difficulty for not pursuing questions of the existence and properties of an equilibrium set of prices is indicated by our example of the price of butter. General equilibrium analysis is designed to trace out the effects of one price change on others; and, as we saw in the butter example, its conclusions tend to read more like a catalogue than a simplifying theory. We can trace the effects of a rise in the price of butter, but these are so numerous that it is not easy to see whether wage earners will be better or worse off. Some will find their economic positions improved if their incomes rise with the price of butter; others who consume butter will be worse off. Statements that are both useful and succinct are often not the outcome of a very general analysis.

These comments on the complexity of general equilibrium analysis are not intended as criticisms of attempts to model the interdependence of many markets. Indeed, whatever we do to develop a simpler model of the economy will in some respects be a very poor relation of general equilibrium theory. Where modern general equilibrium theory has weaknesses (it often makes unrealistic assumptions about peoples' expectations, for example) our theories will also be weak – unless the view is taken that, by glossing over the details of many cross-relations between different markets at different times and in different places, the 'law of averages' cancels out errors of diverse kinds caused by unrealistic assumptions. Such an optimistic view is hard to support by detailed analysis, and we shall not pursue it. We can only hope to gain advantages in exposition and understanding from simplifications, without paying too high a price by ignoring the complexities of reality for which general equilibrium analysis tries to account.

A general model of the economy that involves all kinds of inter-relations between demands and supplies of different goods will take account of three real-world phenomena that we shall ignore completely. In our models there is no foreign trade; the economy is closed. Second, we shall not include a financial sector in our analysis. We shall mention money as a unit of account, but only in the Keynesian theory of Chapter 10 will money have any more important role. Third, we shall ignore the activities of the government except in so far as a scheme of rules for enforcing contracts and protecting property rights is necessary in a capitalist economy. Only when we discuss the role of pension funds in accumulating savings (Chapter 5) and mechanisms for ensuring full employment

(Chapter 6) shall we refer to any of the activities of the state in a modern mixed economy. These simplifications will enable us to keep track more easily of the main themes of functional distribution theory.

MACROECONOMICS

Even though we are ignoring the features mentioned in the previous paragraph, we still have the task of simplifying general equilibrium theory to reach conclusions on the forces determining the functional distribution of the product. Broadly speaking, two approaches have been used by economists. The *microeconomic* tradition has concentrated on market inter-relationships, but it has restricted the analysis generally to two goods or to a single good and a single factor of production or to two factors of production. The *macroeconomic* tradition has tended to play down the role of market forces in allocating goods and distributing income and has concentrated instead on technical relationships and on broad aggregates such as national income, consumption, saving and investment. The macroeconomic approach has not been limited to a two-good model. As we shall see in Chapter 7, the two approaches are not inconsistent, but they do tend to concentrate on different things. For the most part we shall follow the macroeconomic tradition, developing the themes of our first six chapters, which deal with the technology of the economy, savings, investment and the labour market. The microeconomic approach to distribution theory has been presented by Johnson (1973) who has been one of its strongest supporters. He labels some parts of the macroeconomic theory that we shall follow as 'unorthodox' (see Johnson, 1973, pp. 192–204), principally because he believes that the two approaches are inconsistent with one another. We shall see that this is not so, and it is worth emphasising that the two approaches are both attempts to make the general equilibrium model more manageable and that both have valuable roles to play in a full understanding of the working of the economy.

1.3 OUTLINE OF THE BOOK

THE BASIC MODEL

Our model building begins in Chapter 2, which derives the *effi-*

ciency curve for the economy from the specification of its technology. These curves enable us to derive the wage of labour if the profit rate received by owners of capital goods is known. We shall see that the curves also enable us to derive the output of consumer goods if we know the growth rate of the economy. Efficiency curves can be derived in models with very different technical assumptions and with any number of different industries producing different goods, but for simplicity we shall concentrate on models with one or two sectors.

Chapter 3 uses the efficiency curves to represent the *national accounts* in diagrams. This enables us to represent national income (= national product), consumption, investment, wages, profits and the value of capital (i.e. machines and equipment) used in production in a simple way and hence to see the distribution between wages and profits. It should be noted that we shall ignore the rent of land until Chapter 9.

Chapter 4 examines the consequences of the existence of several different methods of production. Each method has its own efficiency curve, and we shall derive a simple rule for finding out which method will be chosen by profit maximisers. The choice of method of production will affect the distribution of income, and we shall see in detail how this is so. We shall discover that the choice of method depends on the profit rate received by capitalists and that the distribution depends on both the profit rate and the growth rate of the economy. These two rates are left undetermined in Chapters 2–4, and in Chapters 5 and 6 we shall argue that their determination can be separated from the analysis of the efficiency curve. A brief (and slightly more mathematical) appendix to Chapter 4 examines the relation between our representation of the technology using efficiency curves and the somewhat more conventional use of a production function.

Chapter 5 considers the consequences of savings decisions made by wage and profit receivers. These savings decisions stem from the individuals' expectations of the future, and so we shall first examine the microeconomics of intertemporal choice. We shall then discover that, if a fixed proportion of each kind of income is saved, an equilibrium relation exists between the profit and growth rates, which can be derived from the equality of saving and investment that is necessary for macroeconomic equilibrium (in the absence of a foreign trade sector and government activity). So, when either the profit rate or the growth rate is known, the analysis of Chapter 5 determines the other.

9

Chapter 6 examines how conditions in the labour market can give either the growth rate (if there is full employment) or the profit rate (if the wage is set in some bargaining process so that the profit rate can be determined from the efficiency curve of Chapter 2). One of these outcomes, in conjunction with our earlier analysis, is then sufficient to determine the profit rate, the growth rate, the wage, consumption output and national income and so to build up the national accounts and determine the functional distribution. Such a macroeconomic theory necessarily makes simplifications of a general equilibrium model, which argues that all prices, wages, levels of output, growth rates and profit rates are determined simultaneously by the forces of supply and demand in all markets. Apart from the convenience of restricting the number of sectors, our main simplification is the introduction of an *apparent* causal

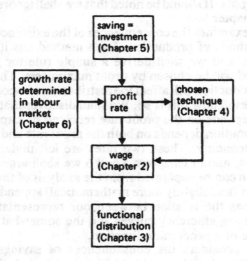

Figure 2 *Structure of the model with full employment*

structure to the model. For example, if the labour market determines the growth rate (Chapter 6), this in turn can be used to determine the profit rate using the equality of savings and investment (Chapter 5). The profit rate then determines the chosen method of production (Chapter 4), and then the real wage is derived using the efficiency curve of Chapter 2. Chapter 3 tells us how to synthesise this information into the national accounts and so to find the functional distribution. Figure 2 illustrates this apparent causal chain. Figure 3 illustrates the chain that arises when the real wage is found in the labour market, so that the profit rate is found from the efficiency curve, the chosen technique from Chapter 4 and the growth rate from the equality of saving and investment.

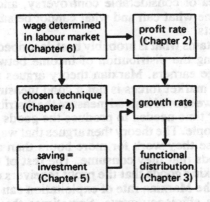

Figure 3   *Structure of the model with fixed wage*

These apparent causal chains arise because we are assuming that there are no 'feedbacks' in the system. For example, in Figure 2 there is no arrow leading from the chosen technique to the growth rate. In Figure 3 there is no arrow leading from consumption output to the wage as we are assuming that there is no feedback in this direction. We shall discuss the assumptions necessary to avoid these feedbacks in the course of the book, but it should be emphasised here that we assume these structures because we assume that the feedbacks are less important than the relationships illustrated in the figures. It is simplifying assumptions that lead us to analyse the distribution in this way; we are not led to these apparent causal structures by any belief that economies actually operate this way. In fact all the variables are determined simultaneously, and our causal structures arise from our desire to reduce the complexities of the economy to a manageable level.

FURTHER DEVELOPMENTS

The rest of the book consists of comments on and amendments to the basic structure built up in the first six chapters. Chapter 7 examines the *marginal productivity theory* of distribution, which is central to the microeconomic approach. This theory states that each factor of production receives a payment equal to the product attributable to the last unit used of that factor. We shall discover that, provided that we make suitable definitions, there is no contradiction between marginal productivity theory and our own. This has been an area of considerable controversy, and this chapter attempts to define what can and what cannot be said concerning marginal products.

Chapter 8 contains what is probably best described as a *Marxian* way of measuring the distribution of income between property owners and wage earners. Marxian theory argues that the wage that arises from market forces is not a good measure of labour's reward and that we should instead measure the distribution according to the labour time needed to produce the goods purchased by each group of people. The theory then argues that wage earners are exploited because they work for more hours than are needed to produce the goods that they consume. The rest of their working time is spent making goods that the profit receivers consume. We shall show that the Marxian rate of exploitation can be calculated simply using the efficiency curve. Sometimes the market wage gives a larger share of national income to wage earners than the Marxian method of measurement indicates, and sometimes the relative sizes are reversed. There is, of course, much more to a Marxian theory of development and distribution than can be contained in a chapter; Desai (1974) discusses considerably more of it in a way that is both succinct and readable by those not accustomed to reading the (often heavy) original literature.

Chapters 9 and 10 examine the consequences of relaxing some of the simplifying assumptions made in Chapters 2–6. Chapter 9 examines the question of *wage differentials* between labourers with different skills. Two cases are taken; and we shall see that, if skills are the result of training, our previous theory will need little modification, whilst, if the skills are inborn, the same sort of analysis can be used, although the equations will become a little more complex. We shall also discover that the distinction between different kinds of labour is theoretically very similar to the distinction between labour and land, and so we can easily adapt our analysis to include *rent*. Chapter 9 ends with a discussion of the differentials between the rents of lands of differing fertility.

Chapter 10 introduces *uncertainty* to the model. We shall first examine likely individual reactions to the uncertain outcomes of investment projects and then introduce a class of *entrepreneurs* whose function is to take risks. From this function they derive *entrepreneurial income*. We shall then use this analysis to build up a Keynesian theory in which there is a much stronger distinction between decisions to save and decisions to invest than in earlier chapters. We shall end up with a model that has an apparent causal structure that is different from that of earlier chapters.

TECHNICAL PROGRESS AND DISTRIBUTION

Chapters 11, 12 and 13 introduce *technical progress*. Such progress allows all the types of income to increase over time, in contrast to our previous discussion in which the different types of income must come from a national product of fixed size. Until technical progress is introduced an increase in wages requires a reduction in profits or rent; in the final chapters of the book it is possible for all of them to increase together. Chapter 11 discusses types of technical progress and then examines the effects of progress on the efficiency curve of a one-sector economy. It is then convenient to define *neutral progress* in terms of the effect of progress on the fraction of national income paid to wage earners and then to classify improvements into *labour-saving* and *capital-saving* types.

This preliminary work leads us to examine the long run behaviour of the economy and possible variations in the functional distribution over time in Chapter 12. We shall discuss the ways in which progress affects the savings behaviour of Chapter 5 and the labour market of Chapter 6. We shall also extend the analysis to allow for choice between different methods of production when there is progress to account for the fact that changes in wages will affect the profitability of different methods and so will affect the actions of 0rofit maximisers. In short, if progress tends to increase wages faster than profits, there will be an incentive to find a technical innovation that economises more on the input of labour than on the input of machines. We shall show that this economising tendency can lead to constant shares of income with wages and profits rising at the same rate.

The analysis of Chapters 11 and 12 is all in terms of the one-sector model as it is easier to keep track of the influence of technical progress when we do not have to allow for changes in the outputs of more than one sector. However, it is possible to make some comments on the influence of technical progress in more

13

complicated models without becoming enmeshed in complicated mathematics. Accordingly, Chapter 13 makes some comments that point to important economic problems but that also indicate that the problem of analysing all the effects of progress in these models is considerably more complicated than in the one-sector model.

NOTES ON THE LITERATURE

Theories of distribution have been central to much writing throughout the history of economic thought; Dobb (1973) provides an historical survey. To a large extent our analysis follows the modern interpretations of Ricardo (1817); see Sraffa (1951, 1960).

The theory and practice of the personal distribution of income have been discussed by Atkinson (1972, 1975, 1976), Pen (1971), Phelps Brown (1968, 1977) and the reports of the Royal Commission (HMSO, 1975). Both the personal and the functional distribution have been discussed by Johnson (1973), mainly from a microeconomic point of view. General equilibrium theory in the tradition of Walras (1890) (and in the more modern mathematical form of Debreu, 1959) has been presented by Arrow and Hahn (1971) and, at a somewhat lower level of mathematical sophistication, by Quirk and Saposnik (1968). The intertemporal aspects of general equilibrium theory have been emphasised by Bliss (1975), who develops the work of Malinvaud (1953, 1961) and Koopmans (1957). These works are mathematical in nature, and Dixit (1977) uses relatively little mathematics to provide an introduction to and review of Bliss.

Distribution, capital and growth theories are closely linked; Wan (1971), Jones (1975) and Dixit (1976) are texts in economic growth. The first named is fairly mathematical. Hahn and Matthews (1964) and Kennedy and Thirlwall (1973) are surveys of the related areas of growth theory and technical progress. Harcourt (1972) provides an introduction to various areas of controversy in capital theory – an aspect of economic theory that has generated a large literature, some of which is mentioned in notes on the literature in later chapters.

Many of the important papers to which we shall refer are reprinted in one or more books of readings of which the most useful are AEA (1954), Hahn (1971), Harcourt and Laing (1971), Newman (1968), Sen (1970b) and Stiglitz and Uzawa (1969). In addition leading authors in the field have produced books of collected papers; see Kaldor (1960b), Kalecki (1971a), Pasinetti (1974), Robinson (1965) and Samuelson (1966b). Many of the references mentioned have large bibliographies, which could be combined into an enormous list of books and articles tracing the development of the subject.

CHAPTER 2
The Efficiency Curve

Goods and services are produced by labourers working with other goods, which have in the past been produced by other labourers working with other goods. For example, labour in the steel industry works on raw materials that are the products of extractive industries, such as coal mining, using machinery, such as furnaces, that is a product of the engineering industry. The coal miners use machinery made of steel, so that the steel industry depends directly and indirectly on many other goods, including its own past products. The inter-relations of production are complex, and so any theoretical structure that tries to mirror all of them will be far from simple. In this chapter we shall derive a summary of the technology in the form of an *efficiency curve* (so called by Hicks, 1973, although others had used it before under various pseudonyms as our notes on the literature indicate). The advantage of deriving an efficiency curve is that we can introduce it into later parts of our theory as a summary of the much more complicated details of the machine and labour requirements in the various industries. In this chapter we shall start with the simplest theory of production and gradually extend the model to allow for more complicated features.

2.1 THE ONE-SECTOR MODEL

The simplest representation of production acknowledges that goods are produced by labour using previously produced goods, so that we are aggregating the whole of industry into a single sector. This assumption will soon appear to be inadequate for many purposes, but it is a useful starting point. As well as having just one type of good we shall also assume that there is only one type of labour, and we shall retain this assumption until Chapter 9, even though we shall soon allow for more than one type of good.

In the one-sector model we shall assume that one unit (say, 1 tonne) of goods is produced by b units of labour using a tonnes of

16

goods. We shall assume that a productive activity of this kind takes one *week* to complete, and we shall retain the week as our unit for the measurement of time throughout the book. It is then convenient to use the *man-week* (i.e. the labour provided by one worker in one week) as the unit of labour. If one labourer works for more hours in the week than another, we define the man-week to be the labour of one of the labourers, and the other works for a fraction or a multiple of a standard man-week.

To complete our specification of the process of production we need to know how much of the *a* tonnes of goods is actually used up during the week; that is, we need to know the *rate of depreciation* of the goods used in production. If this rate is zero, the *a* tonnes will remain intact at the end of the week, ready to be used again in production the following week or available for consumption. At the opposite extreme all the *a* tonnes may be used up, giving a depreciation rate of unity. In practice rates of depreciation are likely to lie between zero and unity; many machines last for many weeks and so have depreciation rates close to zero, whilst most raw materials are entirely used up in the week of production and so have depreciation rates of unity. In our simple model, where we have only one kind of good, we can have only one depreciation rate, which we shall call d.

PRICES AND WAGES

Each man-week of labour is rewarded by the payment of a wage at the end of the week in which it is supplied. In terms of some unit of account (money) this wage is w_m. There is no need for us to discuss the nature of the unit of account as we shall soon see that it is superfluous when we come to discuss real wages and real profits. It is possible to assume that the wage is paid at the start rather than the end of the week, but we shall see that this adds only a little to the complexity of the formulae that we derive and nothing at all to the theory. We shall therefore assume throughout the book that wages are paid at the end of the week.

The money price of 1 tonne of goods is p, so that a capitalist producing 1 tonne of goods has a revenue p and wage costs $w_m b$ for the b man-weeks of labour needed. The a tonnes of goods needed as an input must be bought at the start of the week at a cost of pa, but the capitalist stands to lose only dpa of this since the rest of the goods remain available for use the next week. Thus his profit net of depreciation for each tonne of goods produced is $(p - w_m b - dpa)$, and the profit rate r that he receives on his initial investment of pa is given by

$$r = \frac{p - w_m b - dpa}{pa}$$

We may write this alternatively as

$$p = w_m b + dpa + rpa \tag{1}$$

which tells us that

revenue = wage bill + depreciation + profit

The recipient of the money wage w_m can purchase w_m/p tonnes of goods, and so the *real wage* w is given by

$$w = \frac{w_m}{p} \tag{2}$$

If we divide equation 1 through by p and substitute using equation 2, we have

$$1 = wb + (r + d)a \tag{3}$$

From equation 3 we can derive the equation of the *price efficiency curve*, which tells us the formula for the real wage in terms of the profit rate:

$$w = \frac{1 - ra - da}{b} \tag{4}$$

Figure 4 illustrates such a curve. It is a downward-sloping straight line BA. At point A, $r = (1 - da)/a$ and $w = 0$; whilst at point B, $r = 0$ and $w = (1 - da)/b$. The slope of the line is OB/OA which is equal to $-(a/b)$, and so the steepness of the slope of the price efficiency curve depends on the ratio of the input of goods to the input of labour.

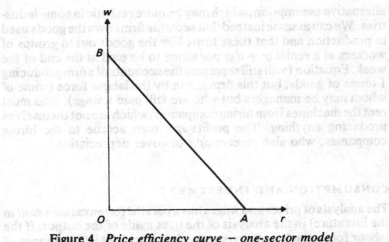

Figure 4 *Price efficiency curve − one-sector model*

TWO COMMENTS

(1) If the wage is paid at the start of the week in which the labour is supplied, the capitalist's initial investment includes the wages that he must advance to the labourers before he receives his revenue. The initial investment is then $(pa + w_m b)$, so that equation 1 is modified to

$$p = w_m b + dpa + r(w_m b + pa)$$

and the price efficiency curve, equation 4, becomes

$$w = \frac{1 - ra - da}{b(1 + r)} \qquad (5)$$

This is no longer a straight line relationship between w and r and is therefore less easy to deal with. We shall meet other price efficiency curves that are not straight lines later in the chapter, and all our future analysis can be adapted to use equation 5 rather than equation 4.

(2) We have assumed that the capitalist purchases the a tonnes of goods that he wishes to use at the start of the week. We can make an

alternative assumption, which may be more realistic in some industries. We can assume instead that separate firms own the goods used in production and that these firms hire the goods out to groups of workers at a rental $(r + d)p$ per tonne to be paid at the end of the week. Equation 1 will still represent the accounts of a firm producing 1 tonne of goods, but this firm is run by the labour force (some of whom may be managers but who are still paid a wage), who must rent the machines from hiring companies, which are not themselves producing anything. The profits rpa then accrue to the hiring companies, who also receive dpa to cover depreciation.

CONSUMPTION AND INVESTMENT

The analysis of prices and wages has a parallel (often called a *dual* in the literature) in the analysis of the uses made of the output. If the labour force employed in some week is L, output is L/b tonnes of goods, some of which may be invested and the rest consumed. The output L/b requires the use of aL/b tonnes of goods as inputs, of which daL/b will be used up through depreciation. If consumption is C, net investment after the replacement of depreciated goods will be

$$\frac{L}{b} - C - \frac{daL}{b}$$

and this net investment will increase the stock of goods available for use in the following week. If g is the growth rate of the stock of goods in use, then

$$\frac{L}{b} - C - \frac{daL}{b} = g\frac{aL}{b} \tag{6}$$

which tells us that

net investment = growth rate × stock of goods used

We can rearrange equation 6 and divide it through by L to give a

20

formula for consumption output per man-week of the labour force (c):

$$c = \frac{C}{L} = \frac{1 - ga - da}{b} \qquad (7)$$

This relation between c and g is the *quantity efficiency curve* and is illustrated in Figure 5 as the straight line DC. At point C, $c = 0$ and $g = (1 - da)/a$; whilst at point D, $g = 0$ and $c = (1 - da)/b$. The slope of the line is OD/OC, which equals $-(a/b)$ and is therefore dependent on the ratio of the inputs needed to produce 1 tonne of goods.

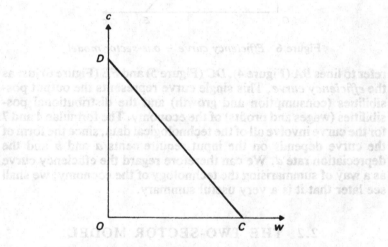

Figure 5   *Quantity efficiency curve − one-sector model*

THE EFFICIENCY CURVE

If we superimpose Figure 5 on Figure 4 using the same scale for w as for c and the same scale for r as for g, lines BA and DC coincide as in Figure 6. **The price and quantity efficiency curves have the same form.** The real wage is related to the profit rate in exactly the same way as consumption output per man-week is related to the growth rate. Mathematically, w is the same function of r as c is of g. We can therefore discard the descriptions *price* and *quantity* and

21

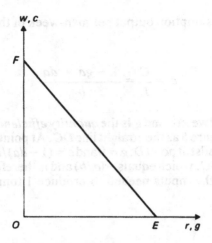

Figure 6 *Efficiency curve – one-sector model*

refer to lines *BA* (Figure 4), *DC* (Figure 5) and *FE* (Figure 6) just as
the *efficiency curve*. This single curve represents the output possibilities (consumption and growth) and the distributional possibilities (wages and profits) of the economy. The formulae 4 and 7
for the curve involve all of the technological data, since the form of
the curve depends on the input requirements *a* and *b* and the
depreciation rate *d*. We can therefore regard the efficiency curve
as a way of summarising the technology of the economy; we shall
see later that it is a very useful summary.

2.2 THE TWO-SECTOR MODEL

The model of the economy to which we shall refer most frequently
throughout the book is the two-sector model chiefly associated
with Hicks (1965). We shall disaggregate the economy to allow for
the existence of two types of goods produced and used in different
ways. We shall assume that one of them is a *capital good*, used in
production but not consumed, and that the other is a *consumption
good*, not used in production. Hicks gives them the convenient
titles *tractors* and *corn* respectively, and we shall follow him in
this. It must be remembered that these names are mere expedients;
they are not intended to imply anything specific about the properties of the goods. Indeed, as in the last section, we shall abstract

22

from the existence of land as an input to production, so that an essential feature of the production of real world corn is ignored.

One tractor, we shall assume, is produced by b man-weeks of labour using a tractors as inputs, which depreciate at rate d during the week. The technology of the tractor sector is the same as that of the whole economy in the one-sector model. A bushel of corn, on the other hand, is produced in a week by β labour using α tractors, which depreciate at rate δ during the week. The symbolism is intentional and convenient (and again borrowed from Hicks 1965); in the corn sector we shall use the Greek equivalent of the italicised Arabic letter used in the tractor sector.

This two-sector model provides a fundamental disaggregation of the economy compared to the one-sector model. It is, of course, unrealistic to suppose that there is only one capital good and one consumption good, but many of the crucial questions in functional distribution theory hinge on the division of resources between consumable goods and those used for investment and upon the possibility that the prices of different goods may react differently if the wage rate or some other economic variable is changed. The principal disadvantage of the two-sector model is that the capital goods (tractors) are used to produce themselves. There is no room for tractor-producing machines that are different from tractors, and so we cannot allow for the interaction of different capital goods. It is not difficult to add extra sectors and goods to the model, except that the notation and the algebra grow considerably, and in fact the addition of extra sectors does not add a great deal to the theory. The greatest step in the development of these theoretical models is the movement from one sector to two sectors.

THE PRICE EFFICIENCY CURVE

If the money price of tractors is p, the money wage is w_m and the profit rate in the tractor sector is r, the accounts per tractor produced will be exactly as in equation 1 for the one-sector model:

$$p = w_m b + dpa + rpa \tag{8}$$

revenue = wages + depreciation + profits

Likewise, in the corn sector the revenue π from the sale of a bushel of corn will cover the wage bill $w_m \beta$, depreciation will cost $\delta p \alpha$ on α tractors, leaving profit at rate ρ on an initial investment of

23

tractors costing $p\alpha$. So

$$\pi = w_m\beta + \delta p\alpha + \rho p\alpha \qquad (9)$$

revenue = wages + depreciation + profits

In principle r need not be equal to ρ, but such a situation can only persist in the long run if there are barriers to entry to one of the sectors, which allow capitalists to make supernormal profits. This possibility is discussed in Chapter 6, but until then we shall assume that there is sufficient freedom of entry to both sectors to ensure that supernormal profits are competed away and hence that $r = \rho$. If r exceeds ρ, resources will move to the more profitable tractor sector, and so the supply of tractors will increase. The price of tractors will then fall, and so tractor production will become less profitable. Fewer resources are used in the corn sector, which reduces the supply of corn and hence increases its price and the profitability of producing corn. The two profit rates will tend towards equality. A similar argument can be used if r is less than ρ, in which case resources will be moved from tractor production into the corn sector, and r and ρ will again approach one another. This analysis appears simple as we have outlined it, but in a more complex model the analysis of the reactions of capitalists to unequal profit rates in each of several sectors producing different goods can lead to a very complex mathematical argument. We shall not pursue this question here, but we should note the methodological point that the analysis with $r = \rho$ is useful only if there are forces that tend to equalise r and ρ if they are initially unequal. Otherwise our analysis will not apply once there is even a very small difference between r and ρ (cf. Samuelson's correspondence principle in *Foundations of Economic Analysis*, 1947).

If we take equations 8 and 9 with $r = \rho$, and divide both of them through by the price of corn π, we have

$$\frac{p}{\pi} = \frac{w_m}{\pi}b + (r + d)\frac{p}{\pi}a \qquad (10)$$

and

$$1 = \frac{w_m}{\pi}\beta + (r + \delta)\frac{p}{\pi}\alpha \qquad (11)$$

24

The ratio w_m / π is the *corn wage*, i.e. the amount of corn that can be bought with the wage of one man-week of labour. Since we have assumed that tractors are not consumed, the corn wage is the real wage as it measures the consumption goods that can be bought with one man-week's money wage. So we may substitute $w = w_m / \pi$ in equation 10 and obtain

$$\frac{p}{\pi} = \frac{wb}{1 - (r + d)a} \tag{12}$$

This in turn may be substituted into equation 11 to give

$$1 = w\beta + \frac{(r + \delta)wb\alpha}{1 - (r + d)a}$$

and this can be manipulated to give the equation of the price efficiency curve relating w to r:

$$w = \frac{1 - (r + d)a}{\beta + (r + \delta)\alpha b - (r + d)\beta a} \tag{13}$$

Hicks (1965) does not deal with depreciation explicitly, and it is often convenient for expository purposes to set $d = \delta = 0$. In this case, where there is no depreciation, equations 12 and 13 simplify to

$$\frac{p}{\pi} = \frac{wb}{1 - ra} \tag{14}$$

and

$$w = \frac{1 - ra}{\beta + r(\alpha b - \beta a)} \tag{15}$$

Where we use equations 14 and 15 rather than equations 12 and 13 the reader may find it useful to carry the analysis through, allowing for positive depreciation rates, and see how little our conclusions change.

THE SHAPE OF THE PRICE EFFICIENCY CURVE

We shall now investigate equation 15 to see how w varies when r varies. First, when $r = 0$, the real wage is $1/\beta$; whilst when $r = 1/a$, $w = 0$. Between these extremes the wage falls as the profit rate increases. This can be shown by writing equation 15 as

$$\frac{1}{w} = \beta + \frac{rab}{1 - ra}$$

An increase in r increases the numerator and reduces the denominator of $rab/(1 - ra)$, so that $1/w$ rises as r rises. However, $1/w$ can increase only if w falls, and so w and r must move in opposite directions. The price efficiency curve must slope downwards as in Figures 7 and 8.

We can also determine whether the price efficiency curve is convex to the origin (Figure 7) or concave to the origin (Figure 8). In Figure 7 point L occurs where $r = 1/2a$ (i.e. one-half of its maximum value $r = 1/a$), and so equation 15 gives at L

$$w = \frac{a}{ab + \beta a} \tag{16}$$

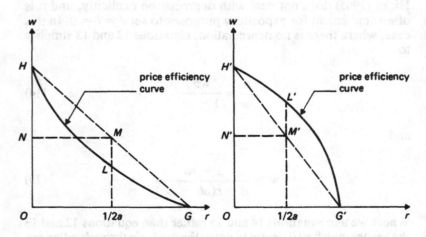

Figure 7 *Two-sector model –* concave case

Figure 7 *Two-sector model –* convex case

Figure 8 *Two-sector model –* concave case

26

L lies vertically below M, which is the midpoint of the straight line HG. The vertical co-ordinate of M is ON, which is equal to one-half of OH. Distance OH is $1/\beta$, and so $ON = 1/2\beta$. So, since L is below M, equation 16 gives

$$\frac{a}{\alpha b + \beta a} < \frac{1}{2\beta}$$

that is,

$$a\beta < \alpha b$$

So, if the curve is convex to the origin, the tractor to labour ratio α/β in the corn sector is greater than the equivalent ratio a/b in the tractor sector.

In Figure 8, L' is vertically above M', so that

$$\frac{a}{a\beta + \alpha b} > \frac{1}{2\beta}$$

and so $a\beta > \alpha b$. If the curve is concave to the origin, the corn sector uses fewer tractors per man-week than the tractor sector. Thus the shape of the price efficiency curve depends on the relative sizes of the two ratios of tractors to labour, a/b and α/β.

The only possibility remaining is that the two ratios are the same, so that $\alpha b = \beta a$. In this case equation 15 reduces to $w = (1 - ra)/\beta$, and so the price efficiency curve is a straight line. Production conditions in the two sectors are identical, and so we have only one distinct method of production in the economy. The two-sector model in this case is similar to the one-sector model of the previous section. For example, if it takes two man-weeks and four tractors to produce one tractor, and one man-week and two tractors to produce a bushel of corn, producers will always be indifferent between producing one tractor and producing two bushels of corn. The money price of a tractor will always be twice that of a bushel of corn, and so there can be no change in their relative prices, just as there is no change in relative prices in the one-sector model.

THE QUANTITY CURVE

The main lesson of the one-sector model is that the efficiency curve can be given two interpretations. We shall now show that the same is true in the two-sector model. The stock of tractors in use at the start of the week is S, the employed labour force is L, the output of tractors is x and the output of corn is ξ. The stock of tractors and the labour force are used to produce corn and more tractors:

$$S = ax + \alpha\xi \tag{17}$$

$$L = bx + \beta\xi \tag{18}$$

Consumable output per man-week (c) is given by

$$c = \xi/L \tag{19}$$

since corn is used only for consumption. Tractors are not consumed but are used to replace depreciation ($dax + \delta\alpha\xi$) and to increase the stock of tractors. If g is the growth rate of the tractor stock

$$x = dax + \delta\alpha\xi + gS \tag{20}$$

From equations 17 and 20 we have

$$x = (d + g)ax + (\delta + g)\alpha\xi$$

so that

$$x = \frac{(\delta + g)\alpha\xi}{1 - (d + g)a} \tag{21}$$

Substituting equation 21 into equation 18 and using equation 19 gives

$$L = \frac{b(\delta + g)\alpha cL}{1 - (d + g)a} + \beta cL$$

and from this we can derive the quantity efficiency curve for c in terms of g:

$$c = \frac{1 - (d + g)a}{\beta + (g + \delta)\alpha b - (g + d)\beta a} \tag{22}$$

28

Once again c is related to g by the same formula (equation 22) as relates w to r (equation 13). The quantity curve and the price curve can therefore be superimposed on the same diagram as in the one-sector model. We can again refer simply to an efficiency curve, which represents *both* the price relation between the real wage and the profit rate *and* the quantity relation between consumption output per man-week and the growth rate.

2.3 AUSTRIAN MODELS

An alternative view of production has been taken by authors in the Austrian school of thought. Rather than emphasising the role of capital goods as we do in the two-sector model, the Austrian tradition stresses the *time lags* that occur between inputs of labour and outputs of consumable goods. A simple example of an Austrian model consists of a *process* that has an input of b_1 man-weeks of labour in the first week and b_2 man-weeks in the second week. This labour produces a bushel of corn at the end of the third week of the process. A capitalist producing a bushel of corn using this process will have wage costs of $w_m b_1$ at the end of the first week and $w_m b_2$ at the end of the second week. He will receive a revenue π from the sale of a bushel of corn at the end of the third week. If the profit rate per week is r, the revenue must be sufficient to cover wage costs $w_m(b_1 + b_2)$, a profit of $rw_m b_2$ on the second week's wage costs and a profit of $(2r + r^2)w_m b_1$ on the first week's wages, which he must pay two weeks before he receives his revenue. The term $r^2 w_m b_1$ arises because the first wage payment requires a profit of $rw_m b_1$ in the second week, and profit at rate r must be earned on this in the third week, exactly in the manner of compound interest calculations. So we have

$$\pi - w_m(b_1 + b_2) = w_m b_1(2r + r^2) + rw_m b_2$$

and since the real wage w is w_m/π, the equation of the price efficiency curve relating w to r is

$$w = \frac{1}{b_1(1 + r)^2 + b_2(1 + r)} \tag{23}$$

An increase in r increases the denominator of equation 23 and so reduces w. Once again the price efficiency curve slopes downwards.

If the economy is growing at rate g, in the sense that the number of processes begun in each week is $(1 + g)$ times the number begun in the previous week, we can calculate corn output per man-week. If the number of processes begun two weeks ago is h, then the number begun one week ago is $h(1 + g)$ and the number started this week is $h(1 + g)^2$. The processes started this week require $b_1 h(1 + g)^2$ man-weeks as they are in the first week of operation, whilst those started one week ago require $b_2 h(1 + g)$ man-weeks. Thus the employed labour force L is given by

$$L = b_1 h(1 + g)^2 + b_2 h(1 + g) \tag{24}$$

whilst corn is produced this week by those processes started two weeks ago, so that corn output per man-week (c) is given by

$$cL = h \tag{25}$$

Combining equations 24 and 25 yields the quantity efficiency curve

$$c = \frac{1}{b_1(1 + g)^2 + b_2(1 + g)} \tag{26}$$

and once again the relation (equation 26) between c and g is the same as the relation (equation 23) between w and r. The price and quantity curves have the same form.

Hicks (1973) establishes this similarity between the price and quantity curves in rather more complicated Austrian models in which the process may have both inputs and outputs occurring each week. Typically, Hicks argues, the level of inputs will be high in the first few weeks and will be reduced after the productive equipment has been assembled. The inputs may then rise in later weeks as the equipment needs repairing. Outputs will follow a contrary pattern, rising after the initial assembly of the equipment and then falling when repairs are needed. Whatever the pattern of inputs and outputs, it is possible to derive an efficiency curve by compounding wage costs and revenues to the end of the process as we have done in our example. Craven (1975) shows a similar result in a two-sector model in which there is a process of production in each sector, each of which has a varying time pattern of inputs and outputs.

MORE GENERAL MODELS

Each of the models that we have investigated involves an assumption of *constant returns to scale*. We have assumed that the inputs required per unit of output are the same however many units of output are produced. If outputs double, inputs must double; if the employed labour and stock of tractors rise from week to week at rate g, the outputs will rise at rate g also. We shall maintain this assumption throughout the book, as increasing and decreasing returns are very much harder to analyse. However, it is possible to show that, in a wide variety of models where constant returns are assumed, the price and quantity efficiency curves are the same. If, for example, there are several capital goods, each produced in its own sector, we need to know the input requirements of each capital good in each sector as well as their rates of depreciation and the requirements of labour. Once these are known we can construct price and quantity equations much as we have done above. We can then express the real wage in terms of the profit rate and consumption output per man-week in terms of the growth rate. Only when we allow for the *joint production* of goods (as when beef and leather are obtained from the same animal) do some problems arise, mainly because the range of growth rates for which positive consumption output is possible may not be the same as the range of profit rates for which a positive real wage is possible. These complications need not concern us here as they do not add much to the theory with which we are concerned, but they do add considerably to the mathematics (see Craven, 1979).

The outcome of this chapter is that the technology of the economy may be represented by an efficiency curve. The efficiency curve is a useful summary of the method of production, for we shall see that it conveys all of the information necessary for our theory of distribution. Economists have often used ways of summarising the methods of production into a single curve or simple diagram. The most usual way is to use a *production function* (see the appendix to Chapter 4) as a way of summarising technical possibilities. Where there is more than one sector a production function is needed in each sector, and soon the geometry becomes impossible and the algebra difficult. The use of efficiency curves, on the other hand, does not lead to greater complication with a large number of sectors. The only difference that arises between a one-sector model and a model with many sectors (or an Austrian model with a complicated pattern of inputs and outputs) is that the efficiency curve is a straight line in the one-sector model but is not necessarily so in the other case. Our task is now to use the efficiency curve in a theory of functional distribution.

NOTES ON THE LITERATURE

Efficiency curves were so called by Hicks (1973). They had appeared before in the literature as factor price frontiers (Samuelson, 1962), optimal transformation frontiers (Bruno, 1969), wage frontiers (Hicks, 1965), $w-r$ relationships (Harcourt, 1972), wage interest frontiers and consumption growth frontiers (Nuti, 1970). Their earliest appearance was in Sraffa (1960) where they are not named at all.

The origin of the two-sector model in the form that we use is Hicks (1965). The Austrian theory of Hicks (1973) is an extension of Hicks (1970), based on some ideas in Kennedy (1968). Burmeister (1974) and Solow (1974) review Hicks (1973) and show the relation between Austrian and other growth models. The model of Nuti (1970) is rather similar to that of Hicks (1973), whilst Craven (1975) extends the model to two sectors. Bruno (1969), Burmeister and Kuga (1970) and Craven (1979) extend the idea of an efficiency curve to models with more sectors and with joint production. The mathematics is increased considerably in complication when these developments are made.

CHAPTER 3

The National Accounts

The efficiency curve derived in the last chapter relates consumption output per man-week to the growth rate and the real wage to the profit rate. In this chapter we shall use the efficiency curve to represent the national income accounts and, in particular, the distribution of income between wages and profits.

3.1 THE NATIONAL ACCOUNTS IN DIAGRAMS

The principal difficulty with national income accounting is that, where there is more than one product, we need some method of aggregation. In our two-sector model, for example, we need some way of adding together a number of tractors and a number of bushels of corn. Each must be converted into a common unit before we can give a single figure as 'national income'. The most obvious way to achieve this aggregation is to weight each good by its market price; for example, if tractors cost £25 each and a bushel of corn costs £15, then when thirty tractors and twenty bushels of corn are produced the national income will be £750 + £300 = £1,050.

However, in our models the unit of account (money) is arbitrary, and it is more convenient to adopt one of the goods as a unit of measurement. In the one-sector model and the Austrian model there is no difficulty, but in the two-sector model we need to make a choice between corn and tractors. Since the real wage is measured in bushels of corn we shall also measure national income as a number of bushels of corn. Tractors are then measured by multiplying them by their own market price and dividing by the market price of corn. In our numerical example each tractor is valued at 5/3 bushels of corn, and national income measured in this way is 30 × 5/3 + 20 = 70 bushels of corn.

We need also to value the non-labour inputs to production, and where these consist of items of different kinds we shall also need to aggregate them. In other words we need to measure the capital input to production on which profits are received by the owners. In a one-sector model this causes no problem. In a two-sector model we could measure the capital input as a number of tractors, but this would be inconvenient for two reasons. First, it is only a special assumption that keeps tractors as the only input apart from labour. We might have a model with several capital goods or one in which corn was both a consumption good and an input to production alongside tractors. We should then have to aggregate different types of goods to measure capital. The second objection is that, if we measured capital as a number of tractors, the measure of total profits, which is the profit rate multiplied by the number of tractors, would also be a number of tractors. This would then not be directly comparable with the wage, which is either a number of units of account (the money wage) or a number of bushels of corn (the real wage). To compare like with like, as we must when examining the distribution between wages and profits, we would need to convert profits measured as a number of tractors into an equivalent number of units of account or bushels of corn.

In an Austrian model the non-labour inputs in any week consist of part-used processes inherited from previous weeks. These can be sold by one capitalist to another and so have a market price. Thus the capital input can be valued in units of account, and in terms of bushels of corn by dividing by the market price of corn.

We shall therefore adopt the convention that national income, the capital input and profits are all measured in real terms; that is, they are all measured as a number of tonnes of goods in the one-sector model or as a number of bushels of corn in the two-sector and Austrian models.

Net national income produced in a week is Y, the value of the capital input used is K and the labour force is L man-weeks. Two identities are familiar from basic national accounting. First, net national income is equal to the sum of wages (real wages as we are measuring everything in terms of the consumption good) plus the sum of profits. The wage bill for the whole economy is wL; and if the profit rate is r, total profits will be rK. So we have

$$Y \equiv wL + rK \qquad (27)$$

Second, Y also measures net national product, which consists of consumption output plus net investment. Total consumption output is cL, and net investment is the growth in the capital stock gK.

So we have

$$Y \equiv cL + gK \tag{28}$$

Identities involving gross national income and gross national product must include a term for depreciation on the right hand sides of formulae 27 and 28, as we must then include gross profits (rK plus earnings to cover depreciation) and gross investment (gK plus replacement of depreciated goods) instead of the net figures. We shall work with net profits and net investment, as the former measures the value of capitalists' incomes given that the value of their property remains the same (which is a common definition of the income of an individual) and that the latter measures the potential for growth. However, the gross figures may be more useful for some purposes. The capitalists actually receive payments of gross profits, so that the earnings to cover depreciation help to increase their liquidity in the sense that they are free to spend it on what they will. If they do choose to spend their depreciation allowances on corn rather than on replacement tractors, the tractor stock will shrink, and national income will be lower in the future. Gross national product is the actual output of the economy in the week and therefore is a determinant of employment. If capitalists do not replace depreciated tractors, there will be less employment in the tractor sector.

The accounting identities can be put together to yield

$$wL + rK = cL + gK$$

and so

$$k = \frac{K}{L} = \frac{c - w}{r - g} \tag{29}$$

where we denote the ratio of capital to labour K/L by k. Also, using formulae 28 and 29 we have

$$y = \frac{Y}{L} = c + g \frac{c - w}{r - g} = \frac{rc - gw}{r - g}$$

where y is net national income (or net national product) per man-week. It is convenient to use these per man-week terms k and y rather than their total counterparts K and Y, and we shall do so hereafter.

We have seen in the previous chapter that, in each of our models, w is a function of r and c is a function of g and that both of these functions are described by the efficiency curve for the technology. Until Chapters 5 and 6 we shall not concern ourselves with the determination of r and g but shall treat them as given. Much of the debate on functional theories of distribution has been concerned with the forces influencing the growth and profit rates, and we shall review this debate later. In order to do so we shall need the tools of both this chapter and the next, in which we shall also treat r and g as given.

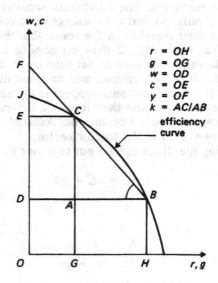

$r = OH$
$g = OG$
$w = OD$
$c = OE$
$y = OF$
$k = AC/AB$

efficiency curve

Figure 9 *The national accounts*

For any values of r and g, w and c are determined from the efficiency curve as in Figure 9. The profit rate is OH, so that the real wage is OD; the growth rate is OG, so that consumption output per man-week is OE. The ratio of capital to labour, k, given by equation 29 is then AC ($= c - w$) divided by AB ($= r - g$), which is

36

the tangent of angle ABC. Profits per man-week are rk, which is DB (AC/AB). The ratios AC/AB and DF/DB both measure the slope of FB and so are equal. Hence rk is measured by DF. The real wage is OD; and so, from identity 27,

$$y = w + rk = OF$$

Thus national income per man-week is OF, and this is divided at D between the real wage OD and profits per man-week DF. This national income can also be divided at E into consumption output per man-week OE and investment per man-week gk ($= DA$ (AC/AB) $= DA$ (EF/DA) $= EF$). **The national accounts can be represented on the vertical axis of an efficiency curve diagram,** and this is true for any model for which we can draw an efficiency curve.

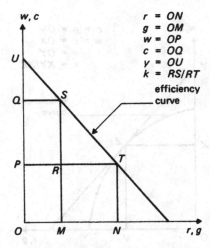

Figure 10 *The national accounts – one-sector model*

Only in the one-sector case can we make any simplification, as we can see in Figure 10, where $r = ON$, $g = OM$, $w = OP$ and $c = OQ$. The capital – labour ratio $k = RS/RT$, which is the slope of the efficiency curve itself, and so y is given by the intercept U of the efficiency curve with the c and w axis. In Figure 9, y would coincide with this intercept (that is, F would coincide with J) only if there were no net investment so that the growth rate was zero.

Our principal concern, i.e. the functional distribution, is represented on the diagram, since wages and profits are to be found there and it is easy to represent a simple measure of the distribution. We can define the distribution in several ways: as the share of profits in income rk/y, as the share of wages w/y or as the ratio of these shares rk/w. It does not matter much which of these we use, but it is convenient to fix on one, and so we shall define the measure of distribution to be the last mentioned, namely, rk/w. If we say that the distribution moves in favour of profits, we mean that rk/w rises. The main advantage of using this measure is that it is directly comparable with the rate of exploitation, which is the measure of distribution used by Marxists. We shall meet this in Chapter 8.

The only difficulty for our diagrams occurs when the profit and growth rates are equal, for then C and B would coincide in Figure 9. In this case, illustrated in Figure 11, the value of k is represented by

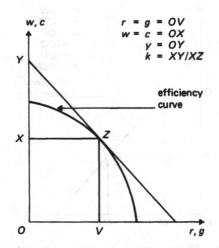

Figure 11 *Tangency solution when* r = g

the slope of the tangent to the efficiency curve at Z. This can be seen to be plausible by allowing r and g to approach one another in Figure 9, so that C and B move closer together. When C and B are very close the line joining them is almost coincident with the tangent to the efficiency curve drawn at B. There is no special significance about this situation except in so far as the condition that $r = g$ is sufficient to give rise to the 'golden rule', which we shall meet in the next chapter. The value of capital per man-week is given by the tangent to the efficiency curve *only* when $r = g$.

3.2 CHANGES IN r AND g

If the given value of r is changed but that of g is not, rk/w will change also. We might expect an increase in the profit rate to increase the capitalists' share of national income, but such an expectation would need detailed investigation since, in general, a change in r has *three* effects on the measure of distribution rk/w: one part of the numerator increases as r increases, and the denominator falls since w falls when r rises (the efficiency curve slopes downwards); finally, k changes when r rises. This last effort is known as a *price Wicksell effect*, after Wicksell (1901), who was the first to recognise that prices change as the profit rate changes (according to formula 12 in the two-sector model), so that the valuation of the capital goods will be different with the new profit rate. If the increase in r reduces k to such an extent that rk falls faster than w falls, the share of profits will fall even though the profit rate rises.

In certain complicated models, involving 'beef and leather'-type joint production, such perverse variations may occur, but we shall confine ourselves here to showing that in the two-sector model such perversity is impossible; an increase in r must lead to an increase in rk/w despite a possible reduction in k. Note that k may fall as r rises, as it does in Figure 12 when r increases from OA to OB. The line DC is steeper than the line DE, but such a change in k can never be large enough to reduce rk/w. The proof is as follows. The total value of the tractors in use is K, which is equal to the price of tractors in terms of corn, p/π, multiplied by the number of tractors in use, S. Now, S depends on the growth rate through equations 17 to 21 but does not depend on the profit rate, and so the change in k depends only on the change in p/π resulting from the change in r. Thus the direction of the change in rk/w when r rises is the same as the direction of change in $rp/w\pi$. From equation 12 we have

$$\frac{rp}{w\pi} = \frac{rb}{1 - (r + d)a} \qquad (30)$$

If r increases, the numerator of equation 30 will increase and the denominator fall, so that $rp/w\pi$ must rise if r rises. Thus rk/w must rise if r rises even though k may fall, as in Figure 12.

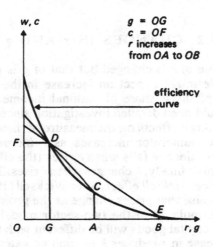

Figure 12

The change in rk/w brought about by a change in g without a change in r is easier to analyse, although the result is not unequivocal. The two possible cases are shown in Figures 13 and 14, where we see that the direction of the change in k as g rises depends on the shape of the efficiency curve. If the curve is concave to the origin (Figure 13), k will rise from the slope of NL to the slope of ML when g rises from OG to OH. In the convex case (Figure 14) k will fall from the slope of US to the slope TS when g rises from OP to OQ. Since w depends on r but not on g, the variation in g will affect the distribution rk/w only through the effect of g on k. Thus rk/w rises when the curve is concave to the origin and falls when it is convex.

This conclusion can be checked by a verbal rather than a geometric argument in the two-sector model. An increase in g requires that more resources are used in the tractor sector in order to produce more tractors and increase the growth rate of the tractor stock. Thus a greater fraction of the labour force must be employed in the tractor sector. If the tractor sector uses fewer tractors per man-week than the corn sector (i.e. if $a/b < \alpha/\beta$), the movement of labour into the tractor sector will imply that fewer

40

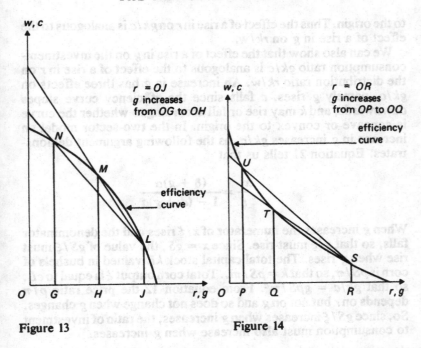

Figure 13

Figure 14

tractors are needed altogether. Some of the tractors used in the corn sector by the transferred labour are not needed when the labour moves into the tractor sector. Thus k will fall if $\alpha/\beta > a/b$. In section 2.2 we discovered that the efficiency curve will be convex to the origin if $\alpha b > \beta a$ (Figure 7), and so the verbal argument confirms the geometric demonstration of Figure 14.

3.3 CONSUMPTION AND INVESTMENT

Although our main concern is with the distribution rk/w, another similar piece of information can be read from the national accounts diagram. The ratio of investment to consumption is gk/c; in Figure 9 this is EF/OE. If r rises and g does not change, gk/c will rise or fall according to the change in k since c depends on g but not on r. Figure 12 shows that k will fall (from the slope of DC to the slope of DE) as r rises from OA to OB if the curve is convex to the origin, and it can be shown that k will fall as r rises if the curve is concave

41

to the origin. Thus the effect of a rise in r on gk/c is analogous to the effect of a rise in g on rk/w.

We can also show that the effect of a rise in g on the investment-consumption ratio gk/c is analogous to the effect of a rise in r on the distribution ratio rk/w. An increase in g has three effects on gk/c, namely g rises, c falls since the efficiency curve slopes downwards, and k may rise or fall according to whether the curve is concave or convex to the origin. In the two-sector model an increase in g increases gk/c, as the following argument demonstrates. Equation 21 tells us that

$$\frac{x}{\xi} = \frac{(\delta + g)\alpha}{1 - (d + g)a}$$

When g increases the numerator of x/ξ rises and the denominator falls, so that x/ξ must rise. Since $x = gS$, the value of gS/ξ must rise when g rises. The total capital stock kL valued in bushels of corn is pS/π, so that $k = pS/\pi L$. Total corn output ξ is equal to cL, so that $gk/c = gpS/\pi\xi$. From equation 12 the price ratio p/π depends on r but not on g and so does not change when g changes. So, since gS/ξ increases when g increases, the ratio of investment to consumption must also increase when g increases.

We can summarise the results obtained in this section and the last in Table 1. The symmetry of these results is a manifestation of the duality between the profit and growth rates and between the real wage and consumption output per man-week. This duality tells us that the effect on rk/w of a change in r is of the same kind as the effect on gk/c of a change in g; and, more generally, it tells us that, although we are mainly concerned with theories of distribution, little extra effort is needed to construct a very similar theory explaining the ratio of investment to consumption.

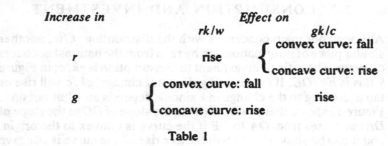

Increase in	Effect on	
	rk/w	gk/c
r	rise	convex curve: fall / concave curve: rise
g	convex curve: fall / concave curve: rise	rise

Table 1

THE ROLE OF SAVINGS

Conventional national-income accounting includes a third identity. In the absence of foreign trade and a government sector, national income is equal to consumption plus savings. In Chapter 5 we shall indicate how savings propensities can be incorporated into distribution theory; but we can remark now that, if wage earners do not save, they must spend all of their incomes on consumption goods, and so consumption output per man-week cannot be less than the real wage. The downward slope of the efficiency curve then tells us that the profit rate must exceed the growth rate (or at least be equal to it). In so far as capitalists consume, $c > w$ and $r > g$; whilst if capitalists save all of their profits (and presumably survive because they also receive wages), $c = w$ and $r = g$, giving the tangency solution of Figure 11. It is therefore possible that $g > r$ only if workers save; we shall examine this case more closely in Chapter 5.

NOTES ON THE LITERATURE

The national accounts have been given in diagrammatic form by Bruno (1969) and Spaventa (1970) and, with $g = 0$, by Harcourt (1972, 1976) and Bhaduri (1969). Hicks (1973) discusses the social accounts (which is his term for our national accounts) but has no diagrammatic representation.

CHAPTER 4

Choice of Technique

We have been concerned so far with the analysis of a single method of production in each of the sectors of our models. We now pose the question of how capitalists choose between methods of production when there are alternatives. To avoid confusion we shall refer to a method of production in a single sector as an *activity*, and to a set of such activities, one in each sector, as a *technique*. Thus it is a technique that has an efficiency curve, and by changing a single activity in a single sector we define a new technique. In a one-sector model the distinction is unnecessary, and we shall refer to each different way of combining the inputs as a technique. In an Austrian type of model a different technique involves a different pattern of time lags between inputs and outputs. Each technique gives rise to its own efficiency curve.

From all the activities available capitalists will choose to use those which are most profitable. To judge the profitability of the activities requires a knowledge of costs − i.e. of the wage and prices of inputs − and of revenues − i.e. of the prices of outputs. When these are known the activities with the highest profit rate will be chosen for use, and the others will be rejected. Put the other way around, no rejected activity can have a higher profit rate than any of the chosen activities. We shall now examine the consequences of this in the three types of models that we have previously examined.

4.1 THE ONE-SECTOR MODEL

In the one-sector model there is no distinction between an activity and a technique. Using the notation of section 2.1, 1 tonne of goods is produced using b man-weeks of labour and a tonnes of goods, which depreciate at rate d. The efficiency curve for this technique is given by equation 4:

$$w = \frac{1 - ra - da}{b} \qquad (4)$$

So if this technique is used, and earns profit rate r, the real wage will be given by equation 4. Now let us suppose that some other technique has been rejected because it gives rise to a lower profit rate when this real wage is paid. If the rejected activity uses b' man-weeks and a' tonnes of goods, which depreciate at rate d', to produce 1 tonne of goods, then the profit made (measured in tonnes of goods) must be less than ra'. So with real wage w given by equation 4 we have

$$1 - d'a' - wb' = 1 - d'a' - \frac{1 - ra - da}{b}\,b' < ra'$$

simplifying this gives

$$\frac{1 - (d' + r)a'}{b'} < \frac{1 - (d + r)a}{b} \qquad (31)$$

The left hand side of inequality 31 is the real wage that the rejected technique gives when the profit rate is r. Thus, from the knowledge that the rejected technique gives a lower profit rate we have deduced that **the chosen technique is the one whose efficiency curve is outermost**. In Figure 15, technique I is chosen when the profit rate is between zero and OA (so that the real wage is between OD and OC), and technique II is chosen when r is between OA and OB.

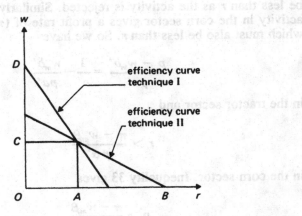

efficiency curve
technique I

efficiency curve
technique II

Figure 15 *Choice of techniques — one-sector model*

4.2 THE TWO-SECTOR MODEL

In the two-sector model a technique consists of two activities, one in each sector. Following the notation of section 2.2, suppose that the chosen technique requires a tractors and b man-weeks to produce one tractor and α tractors and β man-weeks to produce a bushel of corn. We assume for simplicity that the tractors do not depreciate. We suppose that there is another activity in the tractor sector with input requirements a' and b' and another activity in the corn sector with input requirements α' and β'. These activities are rejected because they do not earn as high a profit rate as the activities of the chosen technique.

The chosen technique gives a profit rate r, and so the real wage and the price ratio are given by equations 15 and 14:

$$w = \frac{1 - ra}{\beta + r(\alpha b - \beta a)} \tag{15}$$

$$\frac{p}{\pi} = \frac{wb}{1 - ra} \tag{14}$$

With this price ratio and real wage the profit per tractor produced by the rejected activity is $(p - w_m b')$, and the capital investment needed to produce that tractor is pa'. Thus the profit rate in the rejected tractor-producing activity is $(p - w_m b')/pa'$, which must be less than r as the activity is rejected. Similarly, the rejected activity in the corn sector gives a profit rate of $(\pi - w_m \beta)/p\alpha$, which must also be less than r. So we have

$$r > \frac{p - w_m b'}{pa'} = \frac{1}{a'} - \frac{w_m b'}{pa'} \tag{32}$$

in the tractor sector and

$$r > \frac{\pi - w_m \beta'}{p\alpha'} \tag{33}$$

in the corn sector. Inequality 33 gives

$$p > \frac{\pi - w_m \beta'}{r\alpha'} \tag{34}$$

46

and using inequality 34 in inequality 32 we have

$$r > \frac{1}{a'} - \frac{w_m b' r \alpha'}{a'(\pi - w_m \beta')}$$

This inequality can be rearranged to read

$$(1 - ra')(\pi - w_m \beta') - w_m b' r \alpha' < 0$$

so that

$$w = \frac{w_m}{\pi} > \frac{1 - ra'}{\beta' + r(\alpha'b' - \beta'a')} \tag{35}$$

The term on the right hand side of inequality 35 is the expression for the real wage given by the efficiency curve for the rejected technique at profit rate r. Thus, if one technique is rejected in favour of another because its constituent activities make a lower profit rate, the efficiency curve of the rejected technique will be below that of the chosen technique. Thus in Figure 16, technique I is chosen when the profit rate is between zero and OE and technique II when the profit rate is between OE and OF.

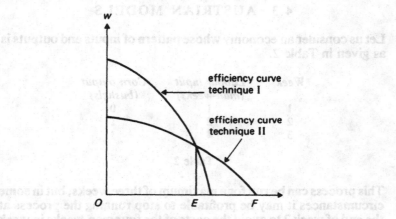

Figure 16 *Choice of techniques — two-sector model*

The argument in the two-sector model is rather more complicated than that in the one-sector model, although the conclusion remains that the technique with the outermost efficiency curve is chosen. In the two-sector model we cannot simply argue that, given w, profit maximisers must choose the technique with the highest profit rate and hence the outermost curve. For our analysis must also account for the price ratio p/π, and we have to ensure that no other activity earns a higher profit rate when its costs and revenues are evaluated using the given real wage *and* the price ratio. In models that involve the joint production of final goods (as in the beef and leather example mentioned in section 2.3) the technique with the outermost curve will not necessarily be chosen by capitalists seeking maximum profits. All that is required for their choice to be an equilibrium (i.e. for there to be no forces moving them away from such a position) is that the rejected activities should earn a lower profit rate at the wage and prices defined by the chosen technique. However, we shall not concern ourselves with the possibility that the outermost curve may not be chosen. We shall always assume that the technique with the outermost curve is chosen, even though we may not specify the sort of technology involved in the economy. We have already seen that this assumption is satisfied in the one-sector and two-sector models, and in the next section we shall show that it also applies to Austrian models.

4.3 AUSTRIAN MODELS

Let us consider an economy whose pattern of inputs and outputs is as given in Table 2.

Week	Labour input (man-weeks)	Corn output (bushels)
1	1	0
2	2	1
3	4	1

Table 2

This process can be run for a maximum of three weeks, but in some circumstances it may be profitable to stop running the process at the end of week 2 to avoid the costs of the four man-weeks in week 3 (and, of course, be deprived of the revenue from the sale of the final bushel of corn).

If the process is used for three weeks and the profit rate is r, the

48

revenue compounded to the end of week 3 will be $[\pi(1 + r) + \pi]$. With money wage w_m compounded costs will be $w_m[1(1 + r)^2 + 2(1 + r) + 4]$, which equals $w_m(7 + 4r + r^2)$. As we saw in section 2.3, the efficiency curve is found by equating the compounded revenues to the compounded costs, so that

$$w_m(7 + 4r + r^2) = \pi(2 + r)$$

and so

$$w = \frac{w_m}{\pi} = \frac{2 + r}{7 + 4r + r^2}$$

If the process is only used for two weeks, revenue at the end of week 2 will be π, and costs compounded to the end of week 2 will be $[w_m(1 + r) + 2w_m]$, which equals $w_m(3 + r)$. The efficiency curve for this pattern of inputs and outputs is thus

$$w = \frac{1}{3 + r}$$

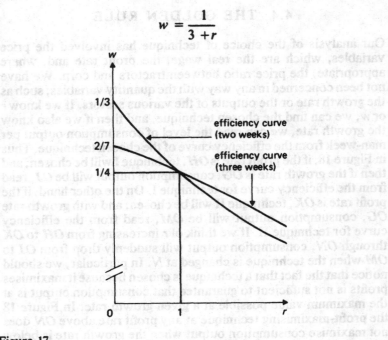

Figure 17

These curves are illustrated in Figure 17, where we see that they intersect when $r = 1$ and $w = 1/4$.

If it is economical to use the process for only two weeks, week 3 is rejected because it adds more to costs than to revenues; $4w_m$ must exceed π, or w must exceed $1/4$. Figure 17 shows that this can only happen when $r < 1$, which is the range for which the efficiency curve of the two-week process lies outside that for the three-week process. Similarly, it is profitable to run the process for three weeks when $w < 1/4$, so that $r > 1$. In this range the efficiency curve for the three-week process lies outside that for the two-week process.

If we change the length of life of an Austrian process, we shall obtain a new technique and a new efficiency curve. We have seen that the chosen technique is the one whose efficiency curve is outermost in this kind of Austrian model. Hicks (1973) demonstrates that the same result is true in all these Austrian-type models.

4.4 THE GOLDEN RULE

Our analysis of the choice of technique has involved the price variables, which are the real wage, the profit rate and, where appropriate, the price ratio between tractors and corn. We have not been concerned in any way with the quantity variables, such as the growth rate or the outputs of the various sectors. If we know r or w, we can find the chosen technique, and then if we also know the growth rate, we can read the level of consumption output per man-week from the efficiency curve of the chosen technique. Thus in Figure 18, if the profit rate is OH, technique I will be chosen; and then if the growth rate is OG, consumption output will be OJ, read from the efficiency curve for technique I. On the other hand, if the profit rate is OK, technique II will be chosen; and with growth rate OG, consumption output will be OM, read from the efficiency curve for technique II. If we think of r increasing from OH to OK through ON, consumption output will suddenly drop from OJ to OM when the technique is changed at N. In particular, we should notice that the fact that a technique is chosen because it maximises profits is not sufficient to guarantee that consumption output is at the maximum value possible at a given growth rate. In Figure 18 the profit-maximising technique at any profit rate above ON does not maximise consumption output when the growth rate is below

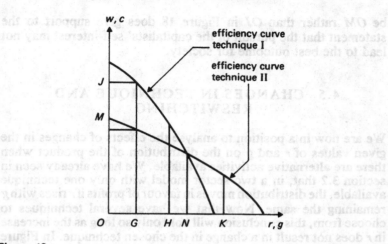

Figure 18

ON. We can, however, be sure of one thing: namely, that if the profit rate is *equal* to the growth rate, the profit-maximising technique with the outermost efficiency curve will also be the technique that gives the greatest consumption output per man-week. This result is known as the *golden rule*. It has been discussed by several authors, particularly Phelps (1961), although his model is different from ours. The golden rule is immediately obvious from Figure 18; for if $r = g = OG$, technique I will be chosen and consumption output will be at its maximum level *OJ*. In that diagram other profit rates also lead to the choice of technique I – any within the range from zero to *ON* will do so – but if there were many techniques, each might be chosen only over a very small range of profit rates. The golden rule will still hold as it depends on the conclusion that the profit-maximising technique has the outermost efficiency curve.

Some authors have used this sort of analysis to claim that capitalism is inefficient, on the ground that national welfare is better served by maximising c given g than by seeking the profit-maximising technique at a profit rate that may differ from the growth rate. Nuti (1970), for example, compares capitalist and socialist systems on these grounds. It is not easy to judge such statements until we have a theory of how r and g are determined in a capitalist system and a theory of how decisions are made under socialism. However, the possibility that consumption output may be OM rather than OJ in Figure 18 does give support to the statement that the pursuit of the capitalists' self-interest may not lead to the best outcome for society.

4.5 CHANGES IN TECHNIQUE AND RESWITCHING

We are now in a position to analyse the effects of changes in the given values of r and g on the distribution of the product when there are alternative activities available. We have already seen in section 3.2 that, in a two-sector model with only one technique available, the distribution moves in favour of profits if r rises with g remaining the same. Now that we have several techniques to choose from, this conclusion will hold only so long as the increase in r does not result in a change in the chosen technique. In Figure 19, as long as r does not move from one side of Q to the other, distribution moves in favour of profits when r rises, and we need no new analysis. We are left with the question of what happens when we change from technique I to technique II when the profit rate is OQ. If the growth rate is OR, the value of capital per man-week (measured in bushels of corn) will change from the slope of VS when technique I is chosen to the slope of US when technique II is chosen. This change is known as a *real Wicksell effect*; it is a change in k brought about by a switch in the chosen technique and hence in the number of tractors that each man-week uses. We can contrast this with the price Wicksell effect, met in section 3.2, which is a revaluation of the goods comprising the capital stock when prices change because the profit rate changes but there is no change in the chosen technique. In Figure 19 the real Wicksell effect will reduce k if we switch from technique I to technique II; and since w is the same for both techniques when $r = OQ$, rk/w will be reduced, so that the distribution will move in favour of wages. The lower part of Figure 19 illustrates how the distribution changes when r changes. The distribution moves in favour of profits as r increases up to OQ; it has a downward jump when the technique changes; and then it rises again as r increases beyond OQ. In Figure 19 the change in technique reduces rk/w as r increases; we shall see below that this is not the only possible configuration.

Before we move on to analyse the possibility that a switch in technique might increase rk/w, note that we need no new analysis to see how changes in the growth rate influence the distribution

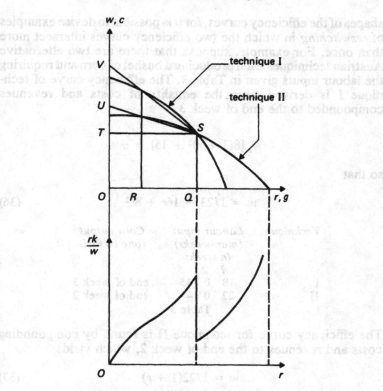

Figure 19 *The distribution as* r *varies*

when there are several techniques available, for in the models being examined the choice of technique is not influenced by the growth rate. Hence, any variation in the growth rate will not change the chosen technique and so will affect the distribution exactly as in section 3.2 where we had only one technique to consider. In that section we discovered that a rise in the growth rate is favourable to profits if and only if the efficiency curve is concave to the origin.

RESWITCHING

In Figure 19 the efficiency curves for the two techniques intersect once, and the real Wicksell effect reduces k and rk/w as we switch from technique I to technique II. This conclusion depends on the shapes of the efficiency curves, for it is possible to devise examples of *reswitching* in which the two efficiency curves intersect more than once. For example, suppose that there are two alternative Austrian techniques each producing a bushel of corn and requiring the labour inputs given in Table 3. The efficiency curve of technique I is derived from the equality of costs and revenues compounded to the end of week 3:

$$w_m[8(1 + r)^2 + 15] = \pi$$

so that

$$w = 1/23 + 16r + 8r^2 \tag{36}$$

Technique	Labour input (man-weeks) in week:			Corn output (one bushel)
	1	2	3	
I	8	0	15	end of week 3
II	22	0	—	end of week 2

Table 3

The efficiency curve for technique II is found by compounding costs and revenues to the end of week 2, which yields

$$w = 1/22(1 + r) \tag{37}$$

The curves are illustrated in Figure 20, although it has been necessary to deform the curves somewhat for clarity. The two intersections of the curves occur when $r = 1/4$ and $r = 1/2$. Checking back in equations 36 and 37 we see that when $r = 1/4$ both curves give $w = 2/55$, whilst when $r = 1/2$ both curves give $w = 1/33$.

If the growth rate is at OE and the profit rate increases from zero, the first real Wicksell effect will occur when $r = 1/4$ and we switch from technique II to technique I. The value of k falls from the slope of BC with technique II to the slope of AC with technique I, and so rk/w falls as illustrated in the lower part of the diagram. When r reaches $1/2$ the chosen technique switches back from I to II, and the real Wicksell effect increases k from the slope of AD to the slope of BD. Thus rk/w has an upward jump when $r = 1/2$. We see therefore that real Wicksell effects can be in either direction, and so the change in the distribution can be in either direction.

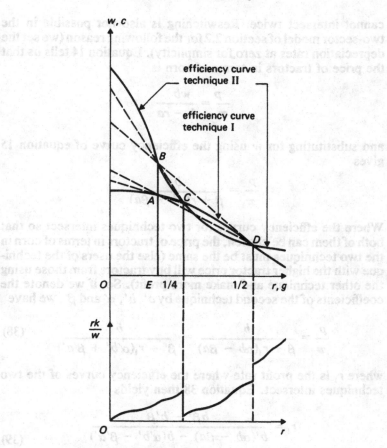

Figure 20 *The distribution with reswitching*

The possibility of reswitching has led, particularly in the 1960s, to a vast literature; we list the high points in our discussion, and Harcourt (1972) gives a fuller list. The main point of controversy was at first whether reswitching could happen at all; and then, when it was shown that reswitching could occur in a variety of circumstances, the debate turned to consider what it meant. We have no space to survey the literature in depth, but let us examine two points a little more closely.

Reswitching is not possible in a one-sector model since all the techniques have linear efficiency curves and two straight lines cannot intersect twice. Reswitching is also not possible in the two-sector model of section 2.2 for the following reason (we set the depreciation rates at zero for simplicity). Equation 14 tells us that the price of tractors in terms of corn is

$$\frac{p}{\pi} = \frac{wb}{1 - ra}$$

and substituting for w using the efficiency curve of equation 15 gives

$$\frac{p}{\pi} = \frac{b}{\beta + r(\alpha b - \beta a)}$$

Where the efficiency curves for two techniques intersect so that both of them can be chosen, the price of tractors in terms of corn in the two techniques must be the same (else the users of the technique with the higher tractor price will buy tractors from those using the other technique and make more profit). So, if we denote the coefficients of the second technique by a', b', α' and β', we have

$$\frac{p}{\pi} = \frac{b}{\beta + r_1(\alpha b - \beta a)} = \frac{b'}{\beta' + r_1(\alpha'b' + \beta'a')} \qquad (38)$$

where r_1 is the profit rate where the efficiency curves of the two techniques intersect. Equation 38 then yields

$$r_1 = \frac{b\beta' - b'\beta}{b'(\alpha b - \beta a) - b(\alpha'b' - \beta'\alpha')} \qquad (39)$$

The value of r_1 is uniquely determined by equation 39, and so no two techniques can exhibit reswitching. If there are more than two techniques, we can take each pair in turn and reach the same conclusion.

It should be noted that this conclusion is not the same as that reached by Hicks in Chapter 13 of *Capital and Growth* (1965) where he develops the two-sector model. In contrast to our model, Hicks assumes that each technique produces and uses a different type of tractor, so that the tractors produced in technique I cannot be used in either activity of technique II. It is then meaningless to say that the price of tractors must be the same in the two techniques when the efficiency curves intersect. We cannot argue that the two types of tractors will have equal prices, since the users of type II tractors cannot be tempted by any price advantage to use type I tractors in the activities of technique II. There are thus no forces equalising tractor prices, and our above analysis fails. In Hicks' version of the two-sector model, with different types of tractors in the two techniques, reswitching is possible; in our version of the two-sector model each technique produces tractors of identical specification, and reswitching is not possible.

Despite the fact that certain simple models cannot exhibit reswitching, numerous more complicated examples have been put forward to show that efficiency curves can intersect several times. Our Austrian example (which is very similar to that of Samuelson, 1966a) is one such, and Bruno, Burmeister and Sheshinski (1966) show that we need only make corn an input to production for the two-sector model to give rise to reswitching with suitably chosen input coefficients.

DOES RESWITCHING MATTER?

Intuitively, it is an agreement with simple economic reasoning that, as the wage rises, profit maximisers will wish to economise on labour by using a less 'labour-intensive' technique. Thus in Figure 19, technique I can be said to be less labour-intensive than technique II because technique I is chosen when the real wage is high. But we cannot say the same in Figure 20, since technique II is chosen at the highest and lowest real wages and technique I in between. Thus, technique II is both less and more labour-intensive than technique I, and so these intuitive arguments are misleading. When there is reswitching it is not possible to say that one technique is more labour-intensive than another solely on the basis of the ranges of the wage at which the techniques are chosen.

The intuitive argument fails because the idea of labour intensity is not defined. To define labour intensity we need some measure of both labour and capital inputs, and we have seen that when more than one good is used as an input we must measure them in some common unit, such as money or corn. However, the capital input is then subject to price Wicksell effects since the prices used for aggregation change when the profit rate changes. Thus, it is necessary to use a measurement of labour intensity that changes as the rate of profit changes; there is no physical attribute of a technique that can be rigorously used as a way of measuring labour intensity in our intuitive argument.

Much of the controversy in capital theory has arisen in this area, but it must be said that the possibility of reswitching causes no problem for our distribution theory. We do not need a measure of labour intensity to represent a technique as we are using efficiency curves for this purpose. We have shown that in the models that concern us the technique with the outermost efficiency curve is chosen, and this rule is unaffected by the number of intersections of efficiency curves. The only consequence of reswitching that we should note is that it causes rk/w to increase when r increases through an intersection of two efficiency curves. In models in which reswitching is not possible rk/w must fall as r increases through such an intersection.

NOTES ON THE LITERATURE

The choice of techniques in a two-sector model has been discussed by Hicks (1965), in Austrian models by Hicks (1973) and in models with more sectors but no durable capital goods by Sraffa (1960).

The bulk of the literature relevant to this chapter refers to our section on reswitching and on the possibility of ordering techniques according to their capital intensity. The problems of defining a value of capital that is independent of the profit rate and useful in economic theory has been a continuing theme of the work of Robinson (1953, 1956, 1959, 1962,1971). See also Champernowne (1953), who devised a 'chain index' for measuring the capital intensity of techniques, Sraffa (1960) and the surveys by Kregel (1976) and Harcourt (1972, 1969, 1976). Levhari (1965) incorrectly 'proves' that reswitching is impossible, and his 'proof' has been overwhelmed by examples of reswitching: Pasinetti (1966a), Morishima (1966), Bruno et al. (1966), Garegnani (1966) and Samuelson (1966a). Levhari and Samuelson (1966) admit the error made in Levhari (1965). Hagemann and Kurz (1976) investigate reswitching in Austrian models.

The appendix to this chapter discusses the production function, which has been introduced to the theory of growth by Solow (1956a, 1956b) and Swan (1956). Properties of production functions are found in textbooks on growth theory; see, for example, Allen (1967), Ferguson (1969), Jones (1975) and Wan (1971). The possibility of reswitching prevents the use of a single production function in multisectoral models; Samuelson (1962) attempts to develop a 'surrogate' production function for two-sector models, but Garegnani (1970) shows that Samuelson assumes (in our notation) that $a/b = \alpha/\beta$ and so does not extend the one-sector model in the way that he claims. Most neoclassical writers now argue (cf. Johnson, 1973; Bliss, 1975) that aggregation is unnecessary; each sector has its own production function. The simplest example with more than one production function is the two-sector model of Uzawa (1961), Solow (1961) and Hahn (1965). It is easier to generalise efficiency curves for use in multisectoral models than to use a production function in each sector since the efficiency curve can still be represented in a two-dimensional diagram.

APPENDIX: THE PRODUCTION FUNCTION IN A ONE-SECTOR MODEL

This appendix requires the use of a certain amount of calculus. The material presented is not essential to the main theme of our argument; it is intended to show the relation between our approach and another way of representing the technology of the economy.

Many treatments of distribution theory concentrate on the one-sector model and use a production function to describe the relation between inputs and outputs. In such a function the output of goods depends upon the inputs of labour and goods, and users of production functions concentrate more upon the form of the function than upon the individual input requirements on which we focused our attention in section 2.1. The use of a production function is in some ways superior to our own approach in the one-sector model (particularly when the number of available techniques is assumed to be large) for then we can concentrate on the form of a fairly simple function rather than on a large number of combinations of input requirements a and b.

The production function specifies the techniques available for the production of 1 tonne of goods. For example, if it is possible to produce 1 tonne using b man-weeks and a tonnes of goods, and if a and b can take on the values given in Table 4, it will be convenient to summarise the available techniques as the *production function ab* $= 1$. If a and b can vary continuously, the possible techniques will be infinite in number, or *dense* as it is convenient to say. A considerable literature has grown up in capital theory assuming

Technique	a (tonnes)	b (man-weeks)
I	1	1
II	2	1/2
III	3	1/3
IV	7/2	2/7

Table 4

that the available techniques are dense, but we shall treat it simply as a limiting case of our theory as the number of available techniques rises. As the number of techniques increases, it is likely that the intersections between their efficiency curves will crowd in on one another, and it will become more difficult to separate the distributional changes caused by variations in w and r between intersections from those caused by switches in technique.

In Figure 21 we see the consequences of having several techniques. The lower curve, representing rk/w, resembles a saw with small teeth. These oscillations will become smaller as the intersections become closer together, and eventually the curve will become smooth. This smooth curve will slope upwards if the changes in w and r between intersections increase rk/w faster than changes at intersections cause it to fall. Later in this appendix we shall see how the shape of the rk/w curve is related to the elasticity of substitution of the production function.

Let us suppose that the production function for the output of 1 tonne of goods is $a = f(b)$. A technique is then defined by a particular value of the labour input requirement b and the corresponding goods input $f(b)$, and the efficiency curve for this technique is given by equation 4 (with $d = 0$ for simplicity):

$$w = \frac{1 - ra}{b} = \frac{1 - rf(b)}{b} \tag{40}$$

At a given profit rate the chosen technique has the outermost efficiency curve, and so we can find the chosen value of b by maximising w with respect to b, for which the first-order condition is

$$\frac{dw}{db} = \frac{-rbf'(b) - [1 - rf(b)]}{b^2} = 0 \tag{41}$$

60

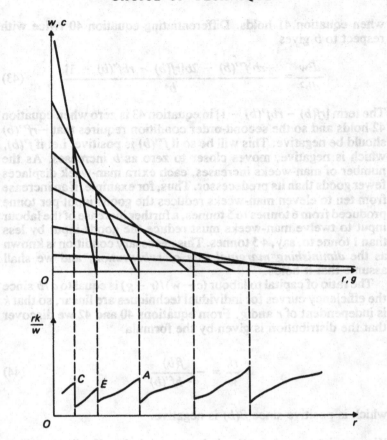

Figure 21

where $f'(b) = da/db$, which is negative since fewer goods are needed on production as the labour required to produce 1 tonne of goods is increased. If this were not so, only the technique using the minimum amounts of goods and labour would be chosen for any value of r. Equation 41 then tells us that the technique with input coefficients b and $f(b)$ is chosen when

$$r = 1/(f(b) - bf'(b))\qquad(42)$$

The second-order condition for the maximisation of w with respect to r is that the second derivative of equation 40 must be negative

61

when equation 41 holds. Differentiating equation 40 twice with respect to b gives

$$\frac{d^2w}{db^2} = \frac{-rb^3f''(b) - 2b[rf(b) - rbf'(b) - 1]}{b^4} \tag{43}$$

The term $[rf(b) - rbf'(b) - 1]$ in equation 43 is zero when equation 42 holds and so the second-order condition requires that $-rf''(b)$ should be negative. This will be so if $f''(b)$ is positive, i.e. if $f'(b)$, which is negative, moves closer to zero as b increases. As the number of man-weeks increases, each extra man-week displaces fewer goods than its predecessor. Thus, for example, if an increase from ten to eleven man-weeks reduces the goods input per tonne produced from 6 tonnes to 5 tonnes, a further increase of the labour input to twelve man-weeks must reduce the goods input by less than 1 tonne to, say, 4·5 tonnes. This necessary condition is known as the *diminishing marginal rate of substitution*, and we shall assume that it holds.

The ratio of capital to labour $(c - w)/(r - g)$ is equal to a/b since the efficiency curves for individual techniques are linear, so that k is independent of r and g. From equations 40 and 42 we discover that the distribution is given by the formula

$$\frac{rk}{w} = -\frac{f(b)}{-bf'(b)} \tag{44}$$

which is positive since $f'(b)$ is negative.

We are interested in the behaviour of the distribution as r increases; thus, we want to know the sign of the derivative of equation 44 with respect to r:

$$\frac{d}{dr}\left(\frac{rk}{w}\right) = \frac{d}{dr}\left(-\frac{f(b)}{bf'(b)}\right) = \frac{db}{dr} \cdot \frac{d}{db}\left(-\frac{f(b)}{bf'(b)}\right) \tag{45}$$

From equation 42,

$$\frac{dr}{db} = \frac{bf''(b)}{[f(b) - bf'(b)]^2}$$

and also

$$\frac{d}{db}\left(\frac{f(b)}{-bf'(b)}\right) = -\frac{b[f'(b)]^2 - f(b)[bf''(b) + f'(b)]}{[bf'(b)]^2}$$

so that equation 45 becomes

$$\frac{d}{dr}\left(\frac{rk}{w}\right) = -\frac{[f(b) - bf'(b)]^2\{b[f'(b)]^2 - f(b)[f'(b) + bf''(b)]\}}{[bf'(b)]^2bf''(b)}$$

The squared terms must be positive, and so the sign of $d(rk/w)/dr$ is the same as the sign of the expression

$$-\frac{b[f'(b)]^2 - f(b)f'(b)}{bf''(b)f(b)} + f(b)$$

So rk/w increases when r increases if and only if

$$\sigma = -\frac{f'(b)[f(b) - bf'(b)]}{bf''(b)f(b)} < 1 \qquad (46)$$

where σ is known as the *elasticity of substitution* of the production function since it tells us the proportional rate of substitution of goods for labour when the ratio of w to r rises by 1 per cent:

$$\sigma = -\frac{a}{b}\cdot\frac{d}{db}\left(\frac{b}{a}\right)\bigg/\ \frac{r}{w}\cdot\frac{d}{db}\left(\frac{w}{r}\right)$$

which can be verified by differentiation of equations 40 and 42.

In terms of efficiency curves we can say that, if the elasticity σ is less than unity, the positive effects on rk/w of an increase in r between intersections will outweigh the negative effects on rk/w that occur at intersections. If the elasticity is greater than unity, rk/w will fall as r rises because changes in rk/w at intersections will reduce the capitalists' share faster than the increase in r between intersections increases it, so that E is below C and C is below A in Figure 21. If the elasticity is equal to unity, the two effects will cancel out, and the distribution will be the same for all r. A production function of *Cobb—Douglas form*,

$$a = b^{-n}$$

(where n can be any positive number), has elasticity of substitution equal to unity, for

$$f'(b) = -nb^{-n-1}$$

and

$$f''(b) = n(n+1)b^{-n-2}$$

and then these can be substituted into formula 46 to give $\sigma = 1$. Much theoretical and empirical work has been done on *constant elasticity of substitution* (c.e.s.) production functions (see Arrow, Chenery, Minhas and Solow, 1961) for which σ is constant for all values of a and b.

CHAPTER 5

Savings and Investment

Our analysis so far is incomplete. We have developed our theory to tell us what the distribution will be when the profit and growth rates are known, but we have not yet discussed the mechanisms that determine those rates. We have extracted as much information as possible from our knowledge of the technology of the economy and from the fact that capitalists seek maximum profits, and in this chapter we shall see what we can conclude from the savings behaviour of individuals. We shall find that the equality of savings and investment that is necessary for macroeconomic equilibrium give us a relation between the profit and growth rates, and then in Chapter 6 we shall discuss the way in which the labour market completes the model by determining one or other of those rates.

5.1 INTERTEMPORAL CHOICE

We argued in Chapter 1 that a general model of an economy would reflect both consumer preferences (demand for goods and supply of labour and other inputs) and the conditions of production (supply of goods and demand for inputs). We discussed there how individuals' expectations of the future play a part in determining the demand for goods to be consumed now. Consider a man who receives an income this week that he wishes to allocate between consumption this week and consumption next week during which he will receive no income other than interest on his savings from this week. We are considering in a very simplified form (two weeks is all that two-dimensional diagrams will allow) the behaviour of someone who is anticipating retirement. The indifference curves (such as *II*) in Figure 22 represent his preferences for consumption in the two weeks. We assume that they have the usual shape, i.e. convex to the origin, familiar from elementary microeconomics. Each curve represents combinations of consumption in the two weeks between which consumers are indifferent, and their

65

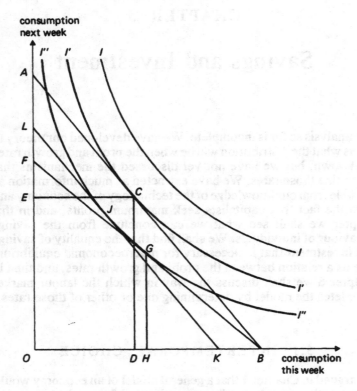

Figure 22 *Intertemporal choice*

convexity implies that, for any given curve, the rate at which consumption now can be substituted for consumption in the future decreases as present consumption increases. The straight line *AB* represents the consumer's opportunities for consumption. If he consumes all of his income now, he can have *OB* this week and nothing next week; if he saves all of his income, he can consume *OA* next week. If his savings yield interest, and if he saves all his income, he can consume more next week than he can consume this week if he saves nothing. The slope of *AB* thus depends on the real rate of return on his savings (we are assuming that his savings do not influence the interest rate as he is one of many small savers). By consuming some of his income in each week he can reach any combination represented by *AB*, and he reaches the highest indif-

66

ference curve consistent with his income at point C where the consumption possibility line AB is tangential to indifference curve $I'I'$. So he decides to consume OD this week and to save DB, so that he can consume OE next week. By this method we can examine intertemporal choices in exactly the same way as the choice between goods in the same week.

The individual's decision clearly depends on the interest rate on his savings; if that falls, OA will be reduced to, say, OF and the consumer's choice will change to point G. The movement from C to G can be decomposed into an income effect and a substitution effect by constructing LK parallel to AB and tangential to $I''I''$ at J. Then KB represents the reduction in this week's income that will leave the consumer on the same indifference curve as the reduction in the interest rate does. The movement from C to J is thus the income effect, and that from J to G is the substitution effect. The latter measures the shift in consumption from the future to the present brought about by the fall in the interest rate, given that he stays on curve $I''I''$. In our diagram HB is less than DB, so that savings are reduced; the substitution effect outweighs the income effect. If the tangency G were instead to the left of DC, the fall in the interest rate would increase saving; if G lies on DC, the individual's propensity to save will be unaffected by the interest rate.

A more general theory of this kind has been developed; it predicts an individual's saving behaviour over several weeks (his lifetime) and has become known as the *life cycle theory of savings*. Such a theory postulates that individuals have expectations of their future incomes and will save and borrow in order to maximise their lifetime utility (or to reach the highest indifference 'curve' in a diagram with as many dimensions as the individual expects weeks of life). For example, a young man may borrow to finance his education or to buy a home, pay back these borrowings in middle age and at the same time save to provide for his retirement or to educate his children. Once again saving and borrowing depend on his view of the interest rate that he will receive on his accumulated assets or that he will have to pay on his debts. Once again a change in the interest rate is likely to affect the proportion of his income that he saves (which may be negative if he borrows or consumes out of capital), exactly as in the two-dimensional example of Figure 22.

A microeconomic theory of this kind is made more complicated by recognising that consumption in any week consists of demands for various goods. Saving behaviour is then influenced by expectations of future changes in the relative prices of the goods that an individual wishes to consume. For example, if food prices are expected to rise relative to those of some luxury goods, a man may wish to save more by reducing his current consumption of luxuries to avoid future starvation. A full theory of this kind must therefore take account of the individual's expectations of changes in relative prices, and we must, in general, consider the price of and demand for every good in every week. If he expects to live for 1,000 weeks and consumes twelve different goods, we shall have a problem with 12,000 dimensions. Furthermore, the theory only deals with one consumer at a time, and there may be many to consider, each with different preferences and different expectations of future price changes.

5.2 SAVINGS PROPENSITIES

The life cycle theory of savings is attractive at the microeconomic level, but it is not much use in an attempt to construct a simplified macroeconomic theory of distribution. We need some sort of approximation to the way in which individual decisions to save and borrow will balance out to give an overall view of the role of savings. We shall follow Chiang (1973) and generalise a little on the assumptions made by Kaldor (1955) and Pasinetti (1962) concerning the saving behaviour of wage earners and capitalists out of their different types of incomes. The workers receive wages, and we shall assume that they save a proportion s_w of their wage incomes. This propensity is independent of the real wage or of any other variable in our model, and so we shall treat it as a given constant. If they have saved in the past, workers will have accumulated funds zL on which they can receive interest at rate i as they can lend these funds to capitalists. Workers save a fixed proportion s_i of their interest incomes iz, and so their total savings are $(s_w w + s_i iz)$ per man-week. The capitalists receive profits at rate r on a value of capital per man-week k, and they must pay out interest iz. Their net incomes per man-week are thus $(rk - iz)$, and we shall assume that they save a fixed proportion s_c of this, so that their savings are $s_c (rk - iz)$ per man-week. All these can be multiplied by the employed labour force L to give the total savings in the economy, but it is more convenient to work in per man-week terms.

Kaldor and Pasinetti both assume that there are only two different savings propensities. Kaldor has $s_i = s_c$ and $s_w \neq s_c$, so that the savings propensity out of wages differs from that out of non-wage incomes, but no distinction is drawn between savings by workers out of interest and savings by capitalists out of net profits. Pasinetti assumes that $s_i = s_w$ and $s_w \neq s_c$, because he assumes that wage earners save a fixed proportion of their incomes without distinguishing interest from wage income.

Given that these savings propensities are designed to represent the complex reactions of consumers to interest rates and price changes in the future, it seems reasonable to keep s_i distinct from s_w and s_c. Pasinetti's argument that s_i is likely to differ from s_c because the two refer to two different classes of people is sound, but there are at least two reasons why s_i may differ from s_w even though both are savings propensities out of income accruing to the same class of people. First, much saving done by workers is in the form of pension schemes, and it is often the case that an individual worker has little or no control over the interest that accrues to such a scheme. The amount of interest retained in the pension fund depends on the number of pensions that need to be paid; and if pensioners spend all that they receive, savings out of interest will depend on their spending and the number of pensions. The existence of compulsory pension schemes may also affect s_w since a worker may be compelled to contribute out of his wages even though he would not make so great a provision for his future if left to make his own arrangements.

The second reason why it may not be reasonable to assume that $s_i = s_w$ is that the personal distribution of income may affect saving behaviour. For example, one man may work overtime, effectively supplying more man-weeks of labour than another, and as he is more highly paid he may save more and thereby accumulate more funds than the lower-paid man. The prospensity of the higher paid to save out of total income (wages plus interest) may be higher than that of the lower paid; and since he earns more interest, the behaviour of the higher paid will increase the propensity to save out of interest relative to that out of wages. For example, if six men each work one man-week and save nothing, whilst two men work for one and a half times as many hours in the week and save one-quarter of their wage plus interest incomes, total wage income is

$$6w + 2(1.5)w = 9w$$

and savings out of wages are $3w/4$. So $s_w = 1/12$. If the six who do not save now have never saved, so that they have no accumulated funds, the propensity to save out of interest is 1/4 since all of the interest income accrues to those with a personal savings propensity of 1/4. Pasinetti's assumption that $s_i = s_w$ may be true of an individual, but it may not be true of the totality of wage earners if there are differences between individuals.

So we are replacing the complicated life-cycle saving behaviour of different individuals by three savings propensities, one for each type of income. Except in special circumstances, such as where G lies on DC in Figure 22, this simplification is likely only to be an approximation, as the savings propensities of individuals depend on the return that they receive on their savings. It is possible to develop our theory under the assumption that the propensities depend on r and g (and also on w and k, which themselves depend on r and g as we have seen), but this does not add much to the principles being investigated. We shall assume that the propensities s_w, s_i and s_c are constants and see the implications for the functional distribution. It must be emphasised that this is only a simplification, and so the results that we shall obtain are simplifications of those which arise in the more general model of the economy outlined in Section 1.2. Johnson (1973) considers that this sort of theory is 'unorthodox' on the grounds that it may conflict with a theory placing more emphasis on market relationships and microeconomic behaviour. There is no such conflict as saving behaviour is a way of representing intertemporal preferences, which must appear in any model of a capitalist economy. We shall examine the relation between our theory and marginal productivity theories, which Johnson uses, in Chapter 7.

5.3 SAVING BY CAPITALISTS ALONE

In order to see the sort of results that we should expect from our savings assumptions let us first assume that both s_w and s_i are zero. The only source of savings in the economy is then saving out of profits by capitalists at rate s_c. We shall assume that workers have never saved, so that their accumulated funds z are zero. So capitalists' net incomes are rk, and their savings are $s_c rk$ per man-week. Macroeconomic equilibrium requires that these savings shall equal investment, which is the growth of the capital stock gk per man-week. So

$$s_c r k = g k \qquad (47)$$

and hence

$$s_c r = g \qquad (48)$$

If either g or r is given, equation 48 determines the other.

Problems can arise when g is given only if s_c is small enough that g/s_c is a profit rate greater than that consistent with at least a subsistence wage with some technique. In Figure 23, r cannot exceed r_{max} since only profit rates below r_{max} are consistent with a wage greater than subsistence (represented by OM). Thus s_c must be at least g/r_{max}. If g is given by ON and $s_c = ON/OP$, then $r = OP$ and technique II is chosen. Consumption output per man-week is OQ, of which wage earners consume OS since they do not save out of wages. Capitalists' consumption per man-week is QP, and so we can see the distribution of consumption as well as the distribution of income.

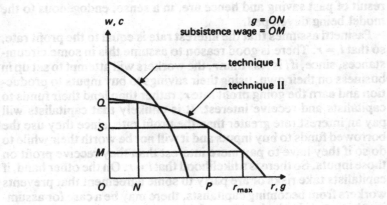

Figure 23

5.4 SAVINGS BY BOTH CLASSES

We should expect to have to replace equation 47 by a more complicated expression when workers save and have funds on which to earn interest and, further, that this more complicated equation would lead to an equation different from equation 48. Pasinetti

71

(1962) shows that, although we replace equation 47 by a more complicated expression, equation 48 remains – and his researches have stimulated considerable discussion, some of which we shall include here.

Assuming that there are three different propensities to save (which is a generalisation on Pasinetti), total savings will be $(s_w w + s_i iz)$ by wage earners and $s_c(rk - iz)$ by capitalists. Thus the macroeconomic equilibrium condition is

$$s_w w + s_i iz + s_c(rk - iz) = gk \qquad (49)$$

If z and i are known, equation 49 will give a relation between g and r since k and w depend on g and r. This relation can then be used in the same way as equation 48 in a theory of distribution.

If we left matters there, the theory would be unsatisfactory for we would have determined r only by specifying the interest rate and the level of workers' funds. We have not provided a theory of the determination of the interest rate, and we have not taken account of the fact that the accumulated funds are themselves the result of past saving and hence are, in a sense, endogenous to the model being developed.

Pasinetti assumes that the interest rate is equal to the profit rate, so that $i = r$. There is good reason to assume this in some circumstances, since, if i is less than r, the workers will attempt to set up in business on their own, using their savings to buy inputs to production and earn the going profit rate r, rather than lend their funds to capitalists and receive interest. It is unlikely that capitalists will pay an interest rate greater than the profit rate, since they use the borrowed funds to buy inputs and it will not be worth their while to do so if they have to pay more interest than they receive profit on those inputs. So there is a likelihood that $i = r$. On the other hand, if capitalists take risks or are party to some agreement that prevents workers from becoming capitalists, there may be a case for assuming that $r > i$. In the last part of this section we shall consider the effect of setting i as a fraction of r, but until then we shall assume that $i = r$.

The simplest assumption that we can use to determine z again leads us to follow Pasinetti and assume that the profit rate and the distribution between wages, interest and profits are unchanged from week to week. Thus interest must remain the same proportion of total profit; and since the stocks of capital goods grow at rate g, each type of income and each type of savings must grow at this rate also to retain the balance between the categories of income. Thus workers' savings per man-week ($s_w w + s_i rz$) must serve to increase their funds at rate g:

$$s_w w + s_i rz = gz \tag{50}$$

Since $s_w w$ is not negative equation 50 implies that g cannot be less than $s_i r$. Furthermore, since z cannot exceed k (else capitalists' incomes $r(k - z)$ would be negative) equation 50 also gives

$$z = \frac{s_w w}{g - s_i r} \leq k \tag{51}$$

In this section we shall assume that capitalists have a positive net income (rather than allow the possibility that it is zero), and so formula 51 contains a strict inequality and can be written as

$$s_w w + s_i rk < gk \tag{52}$$

Thus, if workers were to receive the whole of national income as wages and interest, they would not save enough for macro-economic equilibrium. We shall see the consequences of having equality in formula 51 and the role of inequality 52 in limiting the possible combinations of r and g (and hence the possible distributions) when we discuss 'anti-Pasinetti' theories in the next section.

The capitalists receive an income net of interest equal to $r(k - z)$, and so their savings are $s_c r(k - z)$. The total accumulation of assets in the economy is gk, of which gz is accounted for by the accumulation of workers' funds. Thus the capitalists' savings account for an accumulation $g(k - z)$. This is the amount of the increase in the capital stock that capitalists obtain from their own savings rather than from funds that they have borrowed from workers. Hence we have

$$s_c r(k - z) = g(k - z) \tag{53}$$

and since we are assuming that $k > z$ equation 53 yields

$$s_c r = g \tag{54}$$

73

which is exactly the same as equation 48. Equation 54 has been derived even though workers save, whilst equation 48 followed the assumption that they do not. However, we must remember that equation 54 requires the additional assumption that the distribution between wages, interest and profits is unchanging over time. Equations 54 and 50 tell us that $g > s_i r$ and $g = s_c r$, so that we can assume an unchanging distribution only if the propensity to save by capitalists is greater than that of wage earners out of interest.

Perhaps the most puzzling aspect of equation 54 is that the propensities s_i and s_w have no effect on the relationship between r and g and hence will not influence the distribution. The explanation of this paradox is most easily seen by substituting equation 54 into equation 50 to yield

$$s_c r z = s_i r z + s_w w$$

This tells us that workers' savings out of wages and interest are equal to the extra savings that capitalists would have made had they not had to pay out any interest. If s_w or s_i increases, the value of z consistent with an unchanging distribution will increase according to formula 51, and wage earners' savings will rise. Capitalists' savings will fall as they now have lower net incomes following the increase in workers' funds. The equality of savings and investment is effected by a switch of income from capitalists to interest receivers. There is no need for a change in r, g or k, and hence the share of wages in national income remains the same. However, wages and interest *together* are a higher percentage of national income since rz rises. Thus, there is a redistribution between the two groups of individuals in such a way that total savings are unchanged.

The *assumption* made of constancy in the distribution cannot be used to explain any *observed* constancy, but we can show that, if the workers' actual funds z' are below the level defined by formula 51, they will grow towards that level; for if z' is less than the level in formula 51,

$$z' < \frac{s_w w}{g - s_i r}$$

so that

$$s_w w + s_i r z' > g z'$$

and so this week's savings are more than are needed to increase z' at rate g. Thus, the funds tend to catch up on their equilibrium level given by formula 51. Similarly, if z' exceeds the level of formula 51,

$$s_w w + s_i r z' < g z'$$

Thus, workers' savings are not sufficient to keep the funds growing at rate g, and so the funds fall towards their equilibrium level. The assumed constant distribution is a stable position in that there are forces that bring z towards the level of formula 51.

If, following Laing (1969), we relax the assumption that the interest rate is equal to the profit rate, we can still retain a connection between the profit and growth rates, but it will no longer be quite so simple. Let us suppose that the interest rate is some fraction h of the profit rate, so that $i = hr$. We shall retain the assumption that the distribution is unchanging over time, and so we can replace equation 50 by

$$s_w w + s_i h r z = g z \tag{55}$$

Subtracting this from equation 49 with $i = hr$ gives

$$s_c r(k - hz) = g(k - z)$$

and so

$$g = s_c r \frac{k - hz}{k - z} \tag{56}$$

If g (or r) is given, r (or g) and z can be found as the solutions to equations 55 and 56 given that we can substitute $(c - w)/(r - g)$ for k in equation 56. We still have a connection between g and r, but as it appears in equation 56 it is more complicated than equation 54. However, the expression $r(k - hz)/(k - z)$ can be given an economic interpretation since it is the profit rate that capitalists receive on their own assets. Capitalists nominally own the whole of the capital stock per man-week k, but they have financed z by borrowing from workers, and so their own holding in the firms of the economy is $(k - z)$. They receive profits rk and pay out interest hrz, and so their own incomes are $r(k - hz)$. Thus, the rate of return

75

that they receive on their own holdings is $r(k - kz)/(k - z)$. We can therefore write equation 56 as

$$g = s_c r_c \qquad (57)$$

where r_c is the profit rate accruing to the capitalists on the assets that they have financed from their own resources rather than by borrowing.

The main problem with this analysis is not its complexity, for the principle of establishing a link between r and g via savings and investment remains. However, the use of equation 57 requires that we introduce a separate theory of the interest rate and an assumption that workers do not reject the opportunity to obtain interest by becoming capitalists instead. In the presence of uncertainty we might argue that the difference between r_c and i is necessary because of the greater risks involved in the capitalists' incomes. Interest payments may be guaranteed, or at any rate be more secure than profits as a whole. The risk premium $(r_c - i)$ is then established at the level where individuals are indifferent between a certain return i and an uncertain return r_c, and so r_c is the profit target for risky ventures. We shall examine this further in Chapter 10.

5.5 ANTI-PASINETTI THEORIES

On our way to equation 55 we assumed that the workers' funds are less than the value of capital, i.e. $z < k$. Clearly, z cannot exceed k, for if it did capitalists would be unwilling to borrow the excess funds as they would have no use for them. However, a considerable literature has grown up from a paper by Samuelson and Modigliani (1966) on 'anti-Pasinetti' cases, in which $z = k$ (and in which the interest rate is equal to the profit rate). Capitalists have no income left after paying interest, and so wage earners receive the whole of the national income. Equation 54 need no longer hold, since equation 53 is assured since both sides equal zero when $k = z$. However, equation 50 still gives a link between r and g, since with $z = k$ it yields

$$s_w w + s_i r k = g k \qquad (58)$$

If, say, g is given and there is only one technique available, k and w

will both depend on r, which is the only variable left to be determined by equation 58. Where several techniques are available equation 58 must be solved for each in turn since each will give a different formula for w and k in terms of r. Values of r that are compatible with the given g and the savings propensities can then be found, and a particular value of r arising from a particular technique is possible if the value of r is in the range for which that technique is chosen.

These anti-Pasinetti solutions are interesting not because the capitalists would want to live in such a regime but because, when s_w and s_i are high enough, workers' funds may converge towards k just as z' converged towards the level of formula 51 in the previous section. In these circumstances workers will eventually receive the whole of national income; and although the distribution between wage and non-wage incomes can still be investigated, the distribution between classes is no longer interesting. The class of pure capitalists will tend to disappear, and funds for investment will be provided out of workers' savings both privately and through pension funds. Such an outcome may not be completely unrealistic in an economy where large institutional pension funds and insurance companies dominate financial markets.

We should note that, with given savings propensities, the outcome may not be uniquely determined; it may be possible to have an outcome with

$$g = s_c r$$

or an anti-Pasinetti outcome with

$$s_w w + s_i r k = g k$$

because the value of k varies with r. To see this, consider a two-sector model with the notation of section 2.2, in which $a = 1$, $b = 1$, $\alpha = 1$, $\beta = 2$, $g = 1/3$, $s_c = 2/3$, $s_w = 1/10$ and $s_i = 7/18$. The efficiency curve (from equation 15) is

$$w = \frac{1 - r}{2 - r}$$

and c is similarly related to g. Hence $c = 2/5$. A solution with $r = g/s_c = 1/2$ is possible, for then $w = 1/3$ and $k = 2/5$ so that

77

inequality 52 holds since

$$s_w w + s_i rk = \frac{1}{9} < \frac{2}{15} = gk$$

From formula 51, $z = 6/25$, so that capitalists' incomes per man-week $r(k - z)$ are $2/25$ and workers' total incomes $(w + rz)$ are $34/75$.

Alternatively, if $r = 3/4$, then $w = 1/5$ and $k = 12/25$. Equation 58 holds since

$$gk = \frac{4}{25} = s_w w + s_i rk$$

From formula 51, $z = k$, so that capitalists have no income left after paying out interest. The lesson of this example is that the constraint of inequality 52 is necessary for there to be a solution with $r = g/s_c$, but the fact that inequality 52 holds for some value of r does not preclude the existence of an equilibrium with equality 58 holding at some other level of r. This non-uniqueness is in addition to the possibility that an anti-Pasinetti solution may be possible for each of several techniques.

5.6 CRITICISMS OF KALDOR AND PASINETTI

Tobin (1960) and Johnson (1973) criticise the 'Kaldor model' (i.e. the use of savings propensities in this way to help to determine the distribution) on the grounds that 'once any income-recipient group understands the Kaldor model, it can appropriate all of the social income to itself by appropriate choice of its savings ratio' (Johnson, 1973, page 204). The capitalists can set s_c in such a way that (with a given growth rate) the profit is the highest that is consistent with a subsistence wage; whilst if workers are the first to understand the model, they can set s_w and s_i so that equation 58 holds, and so $z = k$. Even if we allowed that all the members of one class were able and willing to work in concert, it would be unfair to level this criticism at the Kaldor model alone (cf. Kaldor's reply, 1960a), for in any model of general equilibrium a group's behaviour will have repercussions throughout the economy, including indirect effects on itself. The critics are saying that, if a group understands these indirect effects, they will modify their behaviour accordingly. This is a behavioural assumption, which contrasts with all models of competitive economies where individuals react only to the direct stimulus of the markets in which they operate and have no appreciable effects on those markets. The comment that might be made on the two-class approach to the problem is that it simplifies the model to such an extent that the interests of each group can be clearly seen and the outcome is fairly easy to work out. However, this is a virtue of the macroeconomic approach to distribution theory, which enables us to see the main forces at work. If the model were made much more complicated, it would be difficult to see the overall picture and, of course, more difficult to see how collective action by any group that understood the model could change the outcome in its own favour. The analysis of the interaction of co-operating and conflicting coalitions is far beyond the scope of this book.

5.7 INVESTMENT BEHAVIOUR

We have established a connection between the profit and growth rates by concentrating on individuals' desires to save. We can now ask whether a second, *independent* relation exists between g and r stemming from motives for investment. In the model developed so far we can answer this question in the negative, with certain reservations; for when capitalists decide to invest they decide to buy capital goods, and hence they decide not to spend a part of their incomes on consumption goods. This is just another way of saying that they decide to save a part of their incomes, and it would not be correct to argue that savings and investment decisions are independent. Thus s_c reflects the desire of capitalists to possess capital goods rather than to consume.

This argument presupposes that all, or at least most, capitalists are involved in making investment decisions rather than lending their resources (by renting out machines that they own) to a few individuals who order machines and equipment according to their view of the likely profitability. If these few individuals decide the level of investment and the capitalist class as a whole decides the propensity s_c, it may be possible to argue that decisions to save and decisions to invest are independent. However, investors who are distinct from the owners of capital goods are most likely to exist when there are significant uncertainties concerning the outcomes of the processes of production. When these outcomes are certain capitalists may employ managers who are paid wages, but there is no need to introduce a group of people who are able to assess risks and willing to take them. We shall therefore postpone the analysis of a separate investment function and its rather Keynesian implications until Chapter 10.

NOTES ON THE LITERATURE

The simple analysis of consumer choice over time is due to Fisher (1930) and is well presented by Green (1971). Wan (1971) presents arguments on more complicated life-cycle theories – particularly that of Cass and Yaari (1967). Meade (1966a) includes inheritance in the analysis. Britto (1972) links the life cycle hypothesis to the two-class savings model of Pasinetti (1962). Chang (1964) derives Pasinetti's results more simply (as we do) – but see Pasinetti's reply following the Chang paper. Laing (1969) introduces to the Pasinetti model the possibility that the interest and profit rates may differ and derives the result at the end of section 5.3; whilst Chiang (1973) allows for three savings propensities, which is the basis of our own analysis. These papers develop the Pasinetti model, which is itself designed to correct the 'logical slip' in Kaldor's (1955) paper, which, as we have discussed, assumes that $s_i = s_c$. Samuelson and Modigliani (1966), Meade (1966b), Pasinetti (1966b) and Kaldor (1966) discuss anti-Pasinetti theories, whilst Baranzini (1975) shows that Pasinetti solutions (with $g = s_c r$) and anti-Pasinetti solutions can be obtained as different roots of a quadratic equation.

CHAPTER 6
Full Employment and the Wage Bargain

Our savings theory has left us with only one variable to determine. Once either r or g is known the other follows from the analysis of the previous chapter, and the distribution can be calculated using the tools of the previous chapters. In this chapter we shall examine the role of the labour market in the determination of r or g. In another context Hicks (1973) gives a useful distinction that divides those theories of the labour market which determine g from those which determine r. A *full employment theory* is one in which g is determined by the full employment of a labour force growing at a given rate. A *fixwage theory* allows for unemployment and assumes that forces in the labour market give rise to a certain real wage (at subsistence or above) and hence to a value of r that can be read from the efficiency curve. We shall take each of these in turn.

6.1 FULL EMPLOYMENT

Full employment theories assume that the growth rate of the labour supply is determined outside our model by various social and demographic factors. If the supply of capital goods is to grow at the same rate as the labour supply to preserve full employment, g is known. We may ask two questions: first, is it reasonable to assume that social and demographic factors are not influenced by economic variables; second, what mechanism ensures that full employment is achieved?

The first question requires us to discuss the main influences on the size and growth rate of the labour force. These are the birth and death rates and decisions made by workers on such things as whether to work overtime, whether to retire early and whether to stay on at school. We shall later examine the Malthusian theory, in which variations in the real wage are the principal determinants of the birth and death rates, but this leads to a fixwage rather than to a

81

full employment theory. For the present we shall assume that birth and death rates are independent of the real wage. Since we are attempting to summarise a complex economy into a few key variables and relationships this may not be a particularly unrealistic assumption in advanced economies.

The shorter term determinants of the labour supply – overtime, retirement and the school leaving age – are less easily freed from the influence of the real wage. As the real wage increases some will work fewer hours and seek to take some of their increased standard of living in the form of leisure. Others will work more as it is now worthwhile to labour longer to buy more goods. Similar forces will apply at the start and finish of the working life, although statute and custom are clearly at work here too since the school leaving age and the retirement age limit the variations that an individual can make in his working life. Nonetheless, higher wages will persuade some to retire early to enjoy the fruits of their labours, and others will be persuaded by the higher wages that they should postpone their retirement.

If the labour supply is to be independent of the real wage, the positive and negative effects mentioned above must cancel out when all workers are taken together. Of course, when there is less than full employment, overtime will be less, early retirement schemes may be introduced and students may seek places at college to avoid unemployment. These are not our present concerns, however, since we are analysing full employment. Just as when we assumed constant savings propensities in Chapter 5, we must simplify reality somewhat in assuming that a fully employed labour force is independent of the profit rate.

To answer our second question, simple macroeconomics tells us that there must be just enough investment to equal savings out of full employment income if the labour force is to be fully employed. Furthermore, the investment must be sufficient to ensure that the labour force in the next week can be fully employed also. If over several weeks the stocks of capital goods grow less fast than the labour force, a time will come when the principal constraint on the level of output is the supply of some material input or machine. A bottleneck of machines will prevent the full employment of labour. On the other hand, if the growth rate of the stock of machines is greater than the labour supply over a long period, machines will be left idle and capitalists are unlikely to wish to accumulate more. Investment will fall and a slump will set in with its attendant unemployment. So, for continued full employment the stock of machines must grow at the same rate as the labour supply, and the growth rate g is then given.

6.2 THE STABILITY OF FULL EMPLOYMENT

The question then remains as to how the investment demand is to keep pace with the labour supply. The simplest argument is that the government can ensure this by filling any gap caused by the deficiency of capitalists' demand with public investment. The government will then be able to balance its budget by borrowing the savings generated by the multiplier mechanism set in motion by the public investment. Nationalised industries then take the place of private capitalists, and all our consequences will follow provided that the managers of state industries seek maximum profits. Alternatively, the government may rent out publicly owned capital goods to private individuals, again with a view to maximising profits. If the capitalists' demand for some capital good is larger than that necessary to keep pace with the growth of the labour force, the government will need to take steps to reduce their demand, but this is not likely to be a long term problem as we have seen that excess investment will lead to an overabundance of capital goods and hence to a reduction in investment. As long as the government can prevent the fluctuations caused by a temporarily large demand for capital goods, and can prevent long run deficiencies in that demand, full employment can be ensured and the growth rate of the capital stock is the same as that of the labour supply.

Some authors have proposed that price adjustments may tend to ensure full employment. Kaldor (1955) argues that, if there is unemployment, prices of goods will fall due to lack of demand, but money wages will fall less quickly as they are 'sticky' for institutional reasons. Thus, real wages will rise and profits will fall. If a smaller proportion of wages is saved than of profits, the rise in real wages will increase the demand for consumption goods and also for labour, leading the economy back towards full employment. Neoclassical theorists, on the other hand, argue that unemployment reduces the real wage as labour is in excess supply, and so entrepreneurs will choose more labour-intensive methods of production, thus increasing the demand for labour. There are, however, some problems with each of these theories – as we might expect since they are in complete contradiction with one another on the behaviour of the real wage when there is unemployment.

Kaldor's argument does not imply that the economy is stable towards long-run full employment, for the previously unemployed are not taken into jobs producing capital goods, as they would be if public investment were used to stimulate demand, but instead are engaged in the production of more consumer goods. The whole of the adjustment to full employment occurs through an increase in the production of consumer goods. Nothing has been done to increase the supply of capital goods, and future bottlenecks are likely to arise. Put another way, a rise in w must be accompanied by a fall in r, and then Chapter 5 tells us that g $(=s_c r)$ is also reduced, so that the growth rate of the capital stock is below that of the labour force. Without an increase in investment unemployment must eventually set in.

The neoclassical argument reverses the direction in which the real wage moves, but the Kaldor argument shows that this may increase the unemployment since an increase in profits will lead to less spending if, as is likely, $s_c > s_w$ and $s_i > s_w$. The second problem with the neoclassical argument is that the fall in the real wage and consequent increase in r may not lead to the introduction of a more labour-intensive technique. We are concerned once more with an increase in r through an intersection of two efficiency curves, so that the chosen technique is changed. The possibility of reswitching investigated in section 4.5 implies that k can move in either direction as r increases and that the labour used with a particular set of capital goods may increase or decrease as r rises. This criticism of the neoclassical theory is an application of our conclusion that the term 'labour intensity' cannot be defined in such a way that a more labour-intensive technique is necessarily introduced as the real wage falls (see section 4.5).

Both Kaldor and the neoclassicals are concerned with the stability of full employment. The difference between them is familiar from debates between Keynesian and classical economists; Keynesians emphasise the need to increase aggregate demand to reduce unemployment, whilst neoclassical economists emphasise the need to reduce the price of labour (i.e. the real wage) in the presence of excess supply. More complex questions arise when we consider the time that the economy takes to reach full employment under either mechanism. A public sector stimulus to investment or to consumption may be needed if the price mechanism increases employment only very slowly. However, these stability arguments do not affect the general conclusion that, if continued full employment is somehow assured, we can complete our model of distribution provided that the growth rate of the labour force is independent of the real wage. The apparent causal chain is then as illustrated in Figure 2 in Chapter 1.

6.3 FIXWAGE THEORIES: SUBSISTENCE

Subsistence clearly puts a minimum to the wage level that can be sustained. The *Malthusian* argument asserts that any deviation of the real wage from this level sets in motion demographic forces that alter the size of the labour force. We can therefore contrast this theory with the full employment model, which has needed to assume that the size of the labour force is unaffected by w.

The first part of the Malthusian argument is that any deviation of w below the subsistence level leads to a reduction of the available labour force through deaths. The reduction in the supply of labour implies that there is less competition for jobs, and the wage that employers must pay to secure labour will rise back towards subsistence. If the wage rises above subsistence, the workers' condition of life will improve, more food will be available to support more children and so the rate of infant mortality will fall. Other people will be better fed too, the death rate and sickness will be reduced and competition for jobs will increase so that the real wage will be reduced. Thus demographic forces dependent on the real wage will make the subsistence wage a stable position, and the profit rate will be the maximum consistent with a subsistence wage. The apparent causal chain of Figure 3 in Chapter 1 then shows how the model of distribution is completed. We note that $g = s_c r$ from section 5.3 rather than section 5.4 since we do not need to be concerned with workers' saving when their incomes are only just sufficient to keep them alive.

The alternative way in which a subsistence wage may be maintained is through the existence of a *subsistence sector*. It may not be the case that a fall in the real wage causes deaths, but instead workers may be able to migrate to some agricultural occupation from which they can just obtain a living. The manufacturers will have to pay a wage just above subsistence to obtain labour, but they need not pay very high wages provided that the labour force is responsive to wage differentials. The industrial wage will need to be as far above the subsistence wage as is necessary to attract the labour required from the subsistence sector. Then, of course, our analysis just looks at the distribution of income in the capitalised sector; it does not cover those working for themselves in subsistence agriculture.

6.4 FIXWAGE LEVELS ABOVE SUBSISTENCE: BARGAINING

In advanced economies the analysis involving subsistence wages is not relevant. Wages are far above the physical subsistence level, and so we must look for some other explanation of the determination of the real wage. The real wage is determined by two things: the money wage bargain made between labourers and capitalists, and the prices of the goods that labourers buy. The proposition that the power of capitalists relative to that of wage earners is instrumental in setting the money wage is intuitively plausible. Three questions of importance must be answered before we can add flesh to an intuitive skeleton. First, how can we characterise monopoly power as a quantifiable variable? Second, how can such a variable, and its attendant assumption of less than perfect competition, be included in our model? Third, how can we include in the theory the process of *bargaining* between trade unions and large corporations? We shall examine each of these in turn.

The name most closely associated with the relation between monopoly power and distribution is Kalecki (1954, 1971a, 1971b). He argues that the prices charged by firms are determined by a mark-up over average variable costs. The size of the mark-up depends on the monopoly power of the firm; for example, a monopolist may be able to charge a price equal to twice his variable costs (a mark-up of 100 per cent), whereas a firm with several competitors may be able to charge only 1.5 times its average variable costs (a mark-up of 50 per cent). The revenue earned above variable costs must then cover overheads and provide the firm's profits. We need not concern ourselves with the question of which costs are variable and which are fixed — the answer will depend on institutional conditions (such as the ease with which labour can be dismissed) and on the time allowed for the adjustment in inputs following a price change (raw material input may be variable much more quickly than the machine input). The same idea can be used whatever base the mark-up is applied to, for in all cases the mark-up is a microeconomic concept describing the behaviour of capitalists. We can assume that the mark-up will increase if a firm's market share is increased or if the number of its competitors is reduced. Our first question is answered; we have a quantifiable definition of monopoly power.

The second question is far less easy to answer. As we have said, the mark-up is a microeconomic concept, and its level in one market is likely to depend on its level in other markets. The use of the concept in our theory therefore needs some analysis of how the average mark-up is determined. The closest parallel with this problem is the familiar idea of *normal profits* in a perfectly competitive economy. The definition is for a single industry; the normal profit rate is that rate at which no firm is tempted to enter or leave the industry. However, when we consider the economy as a whole we need some other theory to set the general profit rate, which is then the normal profit rate for each industry (subject to some variation for different degrees of riskiness). Similarly, we need some theory to determine the average mark-up in the economy, from which each firm may deviate according to its power of monopoly. Indeed, the mark-up is just another way of looking at the profit rate of a firm, and so the parallel with normal profits is very close indeed.

Even when we have a theory to tell us what the average mark-up will be, the introduction of monopoly power leaves us with another parameter to determine. For example, in a two-sector model each sector may have its own profit rate because each has a different mark-up, so that the price equations with zero depreciation rates are derived from equations 8 and 9 in section 2.2:

$$p = w_m b + rpa$$
$$\pi = w_m \beta + \rho p \alpha$$

Eliminating p/π gives

$$w = \frac{1 - ra}{\beta + \rho \alpha b - r \beta a}$$

The real wage depends on both r and ρ, and so we need to know *both* r/ρ (the relative degree of monopoly between the two sectors) as well as r itself (or some average of r and ρ). In a more complicated model that allowed for every kind of market structure we could allow for barriers to entry in some industries, and allowing for a different profit rate in each sector is a step towards that. It is also a step away from seeing whether there are any general propositions on distribution that can be made in relatively simple models, and so we shall not pursue it further here. We shall only conclude that the microeconomic concept of the mark-up cannot be used to determine the profit rate for the economy as a whole. It may have a role in an investigation of the existence of different profit rates in different industries in a more complex model.

The third question asks whether the overall bargaining power of labourers and capitalists has any role in determining the real wage. It is clear that the relative strengths of the two sides will influence the *money* wage bargain made in the labour market, but the question remains as to whether trade unions are powerful enough to restore *real* wage levels in the presence of rising prices brought about by capitalists' attempting to increase their own share of the national product. A full theory of bargaining is beyond our scope, but we may remark that in such a theory each side is likely to have a minimum for which it will settle and, further, that the outcome of the bargaining process will determine whether the real wage achieved is nearer to the workers' minimum level or to the maximum wage that is consistent with the capitalists' minimum profit rate; and even though bargaining may not establish a fixwage (we might include subsistence wage theories as situations in which labour has no bargaining power to raise the wage above the minimum) the minimum and maximum acceptable real wages put limits on the range of outcomes that any other theory can bring about.

Until we can allow for a separate investment function as discussed in section 5.7, full employment and fixwage theories provide alternative ways of closing the model and determining the distribution. We cannot have *both* a fixed wage and full employment unless savings and investment behaviour are entirely passive and adjust to the levels consistent with both the value of g given by full employment and the value of r given by the fixed wage. This is not possible when savings propensities are the result of individual intertemporal choices.

NOTES ON THE LITERATURE

Full employment has been assumed by many writers on distribution theory; see, for example, Pasinetti (1962) and writers using one-sector models with production functions as listed in the notes to Chapter 4. Kaldor (1955) and Pasinetti (1962) both discuss the stability of full employment in their models. The Malthusian endogenous-population theory stems from Malthus (1798), and many classical writers have assumed or deduced a subsistence wage in their theories. Marx (1867) relies on a 'reserve army of the unemployed' to give a subsistence wage. Hicks (1932) discusses bargaining, and King and Regan (1976) discuss both the monopoly power theory of Kalecki (1954, 1971b) and the effects of trade union power in determining the distribution. Bacharach (1976) gives some game theoretic analysis of bargaining in the labour market.

CHAPTER 7
Marginal Products

7.1 MICROECONOMIC DEFINITIONS

The marginal product of labour is simply defined in the theory of the firm. It is the extra output gained by a firm from the employment of an extra man-week of labour when all other inputs are held constant. Such a change in a firm's inputs involves the use of a different activity of production, because the ratio of labour to other inputs has changed. For example, suppose that a firm uses three tractors and four man-weeks to produce five bushels of corn and considers an increase in its labour input to five man-weeks, which will produce six bushels using the three tractors. The marginal product of labour is one bushel, and the two activities have production coefficients per bushel of corn as given by Table 5. It is the possibility of such a change in activities that enables us to define a marginal product of labour, and this is a useful tool in the analysis of a profit-maximising firm. A competitive firm can do nothing about the prices of inputs that it faces since it has no market power; and so if it increases its labour input by one man-week, its costs will increase by the money wage w_m and its revenue will rise by the price of corn (π) multiplied by the marginal product of labour. A profit-maximising firm produces outputs up to the level at which its marginal cost is equal to its marginal revenue, so that the marginal product of labour is equal to the real wage w_m / π.

Activity	Labour (man-weeks)	Tractors
I	4/5	3/5
II	5/6	1/2

Table 5

A similar argument can be made about all inputs to a firm that can be varied marginally; the price or wage of an input is equal to its marginal product multiplied by the price of the output. For example, a firm will hire tractors up to the point at which the cost of hiring them (or the cost of buying and owning them for one week) is equal to the marginal product of tractors multiplied by the price of the firm's output. So in the tractor sector an extra tractor costs $(r + d)p$ to hire for a week, and the revenue made by using it is p times the marginal product of tractors in that sector. Thus, when the firms are maximising their profits the profit rate is equal to the marginal product of tractors in the tractor sector minus the depreciation rate.

The fact that there may be several sectors, each using an input, implies that each input may have several different marginal products. Our task in this chapter is to see whether the concepts of the marginal products of labour and of other inputs have any meaning in a model of the economy as a whole and, if they have, whether they are of any use in *determining* the wage and the prices of goods and hence the distribution. Can we use the microeconomic idea of a marginal product to help to determine r and g, instead of one of the methods of Chapters 5 and 6?

7.2 MACROECONOMIC DEFINITIONS OF THE MARGINAL PRODUCT OF LABOUR

In the first section we discussed the decision of a single firm faced with the opportunity of employing one extra man-week of labour. We shall now consider the effect on the whole economy of the employment of an extra man-week.

THE ONE-SECTOR MODEL

In the one-sector model the extra man-week can only be employed by switching to a technique that requires a lower ratio of goods to labour as inputs. If such a switch is to occur, the profit rate and the real wage must be at a level at which the efficiency curves for the two techniques intersect, for it is only at this profit rate and wage that the extra labour can be used.

In the national-accounting identity given in section 3.1, i.e.

$$Y \equiv wL + rK \qquad (27)$$

w and r do not change when the extra labour is used if they are at this intersection. Also K, which is just a quantity of goods in the

91

one-sector model, does not change, and so the change in Y consequent upon a rise of δL man-weeks in the labour employed is given by δY where

$$Y + \delta Y = w(L + \delta L) + rK \qquad (59)$$

Subtracting identity 27 from identity 59 gives

$$\delta Y = w\,\delta L$$

and if the extra labour δL is just one man-week, δY will be the marginal product of labour and will equal the real wage w.

The analysis of the one-sector model does not advance our theory much since we have already concluded that the main problem with the microeconomic definition and its use in distribution theory is likely to arise when there are several sectors each giving rise to its own marginal product.

THE TWO-SECTOR MODEL

There are two different ways of using an extra man-week with the same number of tractors in the two-sector model. We shall later examine the consequences of changing the technique in the manner of the one-sector model, but first we shall discuss the possibility of moving labour between the sectors to employ the extra man-week. We shall assume that depreciation rates are zero for simplicity (and also because the symbol δ is now being used to mean 'the change in' rather than the depreciation rate in the corn sector).

The extra man-week can be employed with the same number of tractors by reducing output in the sector with the lower ratio of labour to tractors used and increasing output in the other sector. For example, if $a = 1$, $b = 1$, $\alpha = 1$ and $\beta = 2$, six tractors and nine man-weeks can be employed by having outputs x of tractors and ξ of corn where

$$ax + \alpha\xi = x + \xi = 6$$

$$bx + \beta\xi = x + 2\xi = 9$$

so that $x = 3$ and $\xi = 3$. A tenth man-week can be used by changing

92

the outputs to x' and ξ' where

$$ax' + \alpha\xi' = x' + \xi' = 6$$
$$bx' + \beta\xi' = x' + 2\xi' = 10$$

so that $x' = 2$ and $\xi' = 4$. The marginal product of the extra man-week employed is one bushel of corn and minus one tractor. Consumption output has increased, and the growth in the tractor stock has fallen.

To obtain a single measure of the marginal product of labour we need to aggregate the changes in the outputs of the two sectors. The obvious way is to use market prices at some given profit rate r, so that we are measuring the change in national income Y when an extra unit of labour is used. In our example the price of tractors in terms of corn is given by equation 14:

$$\frac{p}{\pi} = \frac{1}{2 - r}$$

so that the market value of the changes in the outputs measured in bushels of corn is

$$\frac{1}{2 - r}(-1) + 1$$

which is equal to $(1-r)/(2-r)$, which is the expression (equation 15) for the real wage with this technology. Thus the market valuation of the marginal product of labour is equal to the real wage. This result is true for any r for which this technique can be used. A change in r will revalue the real wage according to the efficiency curve, and it will also revalue the marginal product by changing the price ratio between tractors and corn. The two revaluations are equal, ensuring that the marginal product is always equal to the real wage. (Note that we are ignoring our earlier theories determining r and g; we are seeking in this section to define marginal products from the technology of the economy. We shall show later how the marginal products relate to theories used to close the model of distribution.)

We have seen that the payment to labour is equal to its marginal product when the extra labour is absorbed by shifting resources

93

from one sector to the other. We shall investigate an alternative way of defining the marginal product of labour, which involves a change in the chosen technique of production. Such a change can only occur at a value of r at which the efficiency curves for the two techniques intersect since only there will the capitalists consider a change in the technique of production.

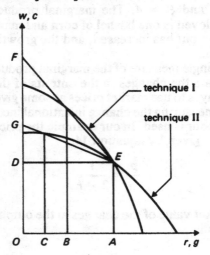

Figure 24

Let us suppose that in Figure 24 the profit rate is OA, so that either technique can be chosen. Initially technique I is used, with growth rate OB, capital per man-week given by the slope of FE (= DF/DE) and national product per man-week OF. When an extra man-week is employed technique II is chosen, with growth rate OC, capital per man-week given by the slope of GE (=DG/DE) and national output OG. The change in national product per man-week is GF, whilst the change in k is ($DF/DE - DG/DE$), which is equal to GF/DE. Since $DE = OA = r$, the change in national product per man-week δy (= GF) is related to the change δk (= GF/DE) according to the equation

$$\delta y = r \, \delta k \qquad (60)$$

The change in total national output Y is

$$\delta Y = \delta(yL) = y(\delta L) + (\delta y)(L + \delta L)$$

94

and so from equation 60 we have

$$\delta Y = y(\delta L) + (r\,\delta k)\,(L + \delta L) \qquad (61)$$

The total number of tractors in use is unchanged, and when the two techniques are equally profitable they must both give rise to the same value of p/π, else the capitalists making the cheaper tractors will undercut the others and make more profit. So the total value of tractors is unchanged; $\delta K = 0$. However, since $K = kL$ the change in L must be compensated for by a change in k. The number and value of tractors per man-week must fall since the number of man-weeks has risen. Hence

$$0 = \delta K = \delta(kL) = (k + \delta k)\,(L + \delta L) - kL$$

$$= (\delta k)\,(L + \delta L) + k(\delta L)$$

So

$$\delta k(L + \delta L) = -k\,\delta L \qquad (62)$$

Using equation 62 in equation 61 gives

$$\delta Y = y(\delta L) - rk(\delta L)$$

and since $w = y - rk$ from the national accounts, we have finally that $\delta Y = w\,\delta L$. Once again, if δL is one man-week, the marginal product of labour will be equal to the real wage. This real wage is that given by the efficiency curves at their intersection E. In more general models where reswitching of techniques is possible the result will be true at each intersection. Each intersection occurs at a different value of w, and at each the price ratio p/π is different, but in every case the marginal product of labour is equal to the real wage.

7.3 MARGINAL PRODUCTS IN DISTRIBUTION THEORY: THE ONE-SECTOR MODEL

These theorems that the wage is equal to the marginal product of labour have been derived by manipulating the various equations and identities involved in the two-sector model of distribution, and it is quite possible to extend the analysis to Austrian and multisectoral models. However, we may well ask whether the result that labour is paid its marginal product places any restriction on the possible values of r and w or of g and c. If such restrictions do exist, we need to take account of marginal products in our distribution theory, and perhaps to use marginal productivity to help to determine the distribution in place of one of our earlier features, such as savings propensities and the labour market. This question has caused a considerable controversy (see the notes on the literature), and to see what the arguments are about we must first consider the one-sector model.

In the one-sector model the efficiency curve of each technique is a straight line, and so the values of capital and national output per man-week are independent of r and g. The value of k is just the slope of the efficiency curve, and y is its intersection with the w and c axis. Suppose that the available techniques have the efficiency curves shown in Figure 25 and that the quantities of goods Q and of labour L to be used in production are given. Then *either* these quantities are compatible with the use of a single technique (whose efficiency curve must have slope Q/L) *or* two techniques must be used, one whose efficiency curve has a slope greater than Q/L and one whose curve has a slope that is less. A suitable combination of these two techniques will employ goods and labour in the given

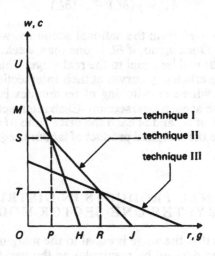

Figure 25

proportions. Let us take these two areas in turn and examine the role of marginal productivity in each.

Suppose first that Q/L equals the slope of MJ in Figure 25. The profit rates compatible with the choice of technique II range from OP to OR; and by the analysis of section 7.2 wage OS is equal to the marginal product of labour defined by using technique II rather than technique I, whilst wage OT is equal to the marginal product of labour defined by using technique III rather than technique II. Thus the wage rates that are compatible with the use of technique II lie between the marginal products of labour defined by moves to adjacent techniques. If the range of wage rates for which technique II is chosen is very small – as it may be when many techniques are available – the two marginal products are very similar in size, and the wage rates compatible with Q and L lie between them.

Now suppose instead that, in order to use inputs Q and L, a combination of techniques I and II must be used (that is, Q/L is between the slopes of MJ and UH). An increase in L, leaving Q the same, causes resources to be moved to the technique that uses more labour per tonne of goods, which is technique II. In the previous section we saw that the marginal product of labour when such a shift is made is equal to the real wage, which in this case is OS since this is the only wage that is compatible with the use of both techniques.

We have therefore established that, if Q and L are given, the real wage will be either determined by (the second case) or constrained by the marginal product of labour. The question remains as to whether this rule carries over to more complicated models.

7.4 MARGINAL PRODUCTS IN DISTRIBUTION THEORY: THE TWO-SECTOR MODEL

Our starting point in the two-sector model is the same: if we are given supplies of tractors S and of labour L to use in production, which techniques can be chosen? Does the specification of S and L constrain the choice of technique; and if so, does marginal productivity feature in the rule relating S and L to w? Let us consider an example with one tractor-producing activity and two corn-producing activities, which gives us two possible techniques. The first technique has $a = 1$, $b = 1$, $\alpha = 1$ and $\beta = 2$; the second has $a = 1$, $b = 1$, $\alpha' = 1/2$ and $\beta' = 3$. All depreciation rates are zero. The efficiency curves are given by equation 15 and are

$$w_{\mathrm{I}} = \frac{1 - r}{2 - r}$$

and

$$w_{\mathrm{II}} = 2\left(\frac{1 - r}{6 - 5r}\right)$$

These curves intersect when $r = 2/3$ and $w = 1/4$. Technique I is chosen when $0 < r < 2/3$, and technique II is chosen when $2/3 < r < 1$. Now suppose that twelve man-weeks and seven tractors are to be used. If the first technique is used, the outputs of corn ξ and of tractors x will be given by

$$ax + \alpha\xi = x + \xi = 7$$

$$bx + \beta\xi = x + 2\xi = 12$$

and so $x = 2$ and $\xi = 5$. The tractor stock grows from seven to nine during the week, so that its growth rate is $2/7$. If technique II is used, the equations will be

$$ax + \alpha'\xi = x + \tfrac{1}{2}\xi = 7$$

$$bx + \beta'\xi = x + 3\xi = 12$$

so that $\xi = 2$ and $x = 6$. In this case the tractor stock grows at rate $6/7$. The given inputs can be used with either technique or with a combination of the two (consider, for example, the use of half the resources in each of the techniques). If both techniques are used, the growth rate of the tractor stock will lie between $2/7$ and $6/7$.

If only the initial stocks are specified, either technique may be used in our example, and so any profit rate between zero and one and any real wage between zero and one-half may arise (subject to restrictions of subsistence requirements). If the choice of technique is to be restricted, we must not only specify the initial supplies of tractors and labour but also know the rate at which the tractor stock is to grow. If g is given, then either a single technique or a combination of two techniques will be used. For example, if g is to be $2/7$, technique I will be used; if g is to be $4/7$, the techniques must both be used, with half of the labour in each case. In the first case the range of possible real wages is known; and just as in the one-sector model, the marginal products of labour involved in switching to another technique place upper and/or lower limits on this range. If a combination of techniques is to be used, the only viable real wages will occur at intersections between their efficiency curves. As we saw in section 7.2 the wage at such an intersection is equal to the marginal product of labour involved in a switch from one technique to the other.

We must therefore conclude that the two-sector model can parallel the one-sector model only if the growth rate of the stock of tractors is given as well as the inputs L and S. In a more complicated model with more than one capital good we must specify the growth rates of all the stocks, and then the same results will hold. In an Austrian model we need to specify the growth rates of the numbers of processes started in each of the previous weeks for which processes now survive.

If the growth rate is given by a full employment theory, the use of specified inputs will restrict the choice of technique, the profit rate and the possible distributions as we have seen. If the wage is given by a fixwage theory, the choice of technique will be determined, and the given inputs will tell us the growth rate and hence the distribution. If the fixwage theory gives a wage at the intersection of two efficiency curves ($w = 1/4$ in our example), the growth rate will not be uniquely determined but will be constrained to be within certain limits (2/7 and 6/7). Finally, if the growth and profit rates are connected by a savings propensity, the use of specified inputs may also restrict the choice of technique. For example, if $g = s_c r$ and in our example $s_c = 4/7$, technique I can be used with the given inputs with $g = 2/7$ and $r = 1/2$. However, technique II cannot be used since, when $g = 5/7$, r must be $5/4$, which is greater than the maximum that is compatible with technique II. If $r = 2/3$, the techniques can be combined with ten man-weeks in technique I and two man-weeks in technique II (and a similar division of the seven tractors) to give a growth rate of $8/21$ ($= s_c(2/3)$). However, if instead $s_c = 6/7$, technique I can be used with $r = 1/3$ and $g = 2/7$, or technique II can be used with $r = 5/6$ and $g = 5/7$. A combination of the two techniques can also be used with $r = 2/3$ and $g = 4/7$. The relation between g and r derived from the equality of savings and investment does not necessarily give rise to an unique distribution when the inputs must be used in specific proportions, but the possible distributions are limited.

It therefore appears that, if the inputs to be used are specified, this information can be used in conjunction with one of the theories of Chapter 5 and 6 to determine the distribution or to limit the possibilities. The marginal product of labour appears in the analysis but only because, whatever the real wage, we can equate it to a suitably defined marginal product. This is an *ex post* idea; the given labour force has a different marginal product according to how it is used. The concept of marginal productivity is not crucial in finding the distribution that is consistent with given supplies of inputs. On the other hand, it is not true to say (as does Johnson, 1973, page 203) that an equation such as $g = s_c r$ is inconsistent with equality of the real wage and the marginal product of labour. A suitably defined marginal product is always equal to the real wage as we have seen. We can therefore conclude that an independent role in determining the distribution may be played by the given supplies of inputs, but the equality of the marginal product of labour and the real wage is not a principle that we need to include separately in our theory of distribution.

The use of a specified input of tractors and labour to determine the distribution is useful in the short run rather than in the long run, for this week's stock of tractors is the result of the growth of the stock in previous weeks. If we are looking for a long run theory explaining how the functional distribution has changed, or why it has not changed, we shall need to know the growth rate in each week, so that we can explain the current size of the tractor stock within our model. For example, if there is full employment and also $g = s_c r$, then, in our example with g given as $1/4$ and s_c as $1/2$, $r = 1/2$ and technique I will be chosen. The inputs of tractors S and of labour L must satisfy the equations

$$x + \xi = S$$
$$x + 2\xi = L$$

and, since $g = 1/4$,

$$x = S/4$$

These three equations can be solved to give $x = L/7$, $\xi = 3L/7$ and $S = 4L/7$, so that the ratio of the tractor stock to the labour supply must be $4/7$. A tractor stock of 400 and a labour supply of 700 is compatible with this growth path, but the tractor stock this week arises because the growth rate is 1/4 and last week's stock was 320 tractors. That in turn arose from a growth rate of 1/4 and a tractor stock of 256 in the previous week – and so on. To explain the size of the tractor stock this week we become involved in an infinite regress (in which the growth rate may change if the labour supply is not growing at a constant rate). For a long run theory it is more satisfactory to explain the growth and profit rates and to deduce from them the chosen technique and the tractor–labour ratio. In a short run theory it is possible to use the inputs as data that do not themselves need explanation and to deduce r or g from them.

7.5 THE MARGINAL PRODUCT OF CAPITAL

The discussion so far has been conducted in terms of the marginal product of labour and the real wage. All of it could also have been carried through by investigating the effects of introducing an extra tractor rather than an extra man-week of labour. Just as the marginal product of labour is equal to the real wage, the marginal product of tractors (measured in bushels of corn) is equal to rp/π, which is the return to their owners. If the stock of tractors is S, the national accounting identity (formula 27) will give

$$Y = yL = wL + \frac{rpS}{\pi} \tag{63}$$

and the introduction of an extra tractor will increase S to $(S + \delta S)$. The wage and the price ratio need not be affected by the introduction of the extra tractor if it is used to change the growth rate or the chosen technique in the same way as the extra man-week of labour in earlier parts of the chapter. Thus the change in Y is given by

$$Y + \delta Y = wL + \frac{rp(S + \delta S)}{\pi} \tag{64}$$

Subtracting equation 63 from equation 64 gives

$$\delta Y = \frac{rp\,\delta S}{\pi} \tag{65}$$

so that when δS is one tractor the marginal product of tractors is seen to be equal to the return to their owners.

Equation 65 can also be written as $\delta Y = r\,\delta(pS/\pi)$ since p/π is unchanged; and since $pS/\pi = K$ we can rewrite equation 65 as $\delta Y = r\,\delta K$. Furthermore, since L is unchanging in this analysis $\delta Y = L\,\delta y$ and $\delta K = L\,\delta k$, so that we have finally $\delta y = r\,\delta k$. We can therefore say that the **profit rate is equal to the marginal product of capital** $\delta y/\delta k$. Considerable controversy has raged over the concept of the marginal product of capital; part of this has been over the use of marginal productivity in distribution theory, which we have already discussed, but disputes have also arisen because k is defined using both the price ratio p/π and the quantity ratio S/L. We have seen that, when the quantity ratio changes but the price ratio does not, the profit rate is equal to the resulting marginal product; but if k changes because p/π changes, this result may not hold.

The only way in which p/π can change is as a result of a change in r, and hence there will also be a change in w. Using the national accounting identity 27 in its per man-week form we have

$$y = rk + w$$

So if k, r and w all change, we shall have

$$\delta y = r\,\delta k + k\,\delta r + \delta r\,\delta k + \delta w$$

and in general δy is no longer equal to $r\,\delta k$. Instead, if S and the chosen technique are unchanged by the variation in r (because r does not change in such a way that the chosen technique is changed), c and g will not change, and we can use the other national income identity (formula 28) in its per man-week form to give

$$y = gk + c$$

and hence

$$\delta y = g\,\delta k$$

The marginal product of capital is equal to the growth rate when that marginal product is brought about by a change in p/π. The price change causes a revaluation of the components of y and k, and the extra value of output is equal to g multiplied by the extra value of capital.

The definition of the marginal product of capital that involves a revaluation of y and k when there is a change in r (and hence involving a price Wicksell effect; see section 3.2) has been the source of much confusion. First, it has no microeconomic equivalent since no physical input is being changed. Second, it gives a result different from, but not inconsistent with, the statement that the profit rate is equal to the marginal product of capital when the latter is defined by a change in the number of capital goods in use. Despite this, confusion arises from two sources: first, the one-sector model is an unreliable guide to the more general cases, yet it has frequently been used in ways that suggest that it can be generalised easily; second, it has been alleged (see Harcourt, 1976) that the introduction of an extra capital good *must* bring about a change in r and hence in$/\pi$. We shall examine these sources of confusion in turn.

The one-sector model is unreliable since it can give rise to a change in k only if the technique of production is changed. In the two-sector model a change in the growth rate can also give rise to a change in k, but in the one-sector model k is not a function of g. Furthermore, with only one good used as numeraire, there is no scope for price changes and revaluations of the goods making up k and y. Critics of the one-sector model have seized on this lack of generality and shown that in more complex models k can be changed by variations in r and the price ratio, and then the marginal product of capital is equal to the growth rate but not to the profit rate (unless the rates are equal as in the golden rule of section 4.4).

At this stage the second source of confusion arises since some authors (notable among their chroniclers being Harcourt, 1972, 1976) have asserted that we must *always* take account of price changes in defining a marginal product. The argument appears to rest on two statements: first, that to use an extra capital good requires a change in technique; and second, that to change the chosen technique requires a change in the profit rate. Neither of these statements is true, for it is possible to use an extra capital good by moving resources between the sectors and thus to change the growth rate; and even if a change in technique is made, the switch can be made at a profit rate where the two efficiency curves intersect. In both of these cases we have seen that the change in the value of capital per man-week equals r multiplied by the change in k.

To sum up, marginal productivity theory is quite consistent with the macroeconomic view of distribution, but it is not a particularly useful tool in establishing what the distribution is. It can be used to express the relation between given inputs and the real wage, but it is not necessary to do so. Finally, the marginal product of capital is equal to the profit rate, provided that we consider physical changes in k through changes in quantities rather than revaluations through changes in prices.

NOTES ON THE LITERATURE

The equality of factor rewards and marginal products has been considered by some authors to be a fundamental feature of neoclassical distribution theory; see, for example, Ferguson (1969, 1972) and Johnson (1973). Kaldor (1955, 1966) and Sen (1963) contrast marginal productivity theories with Kaldor's theory involving savings propensities, and the idea that the two types of theory are inconsistent has been pursued by Atsumi (1960). Harcourt (1972, 1976) strengthens this view by arguing that a marginal product cannot be defined without a change in the profit rate and that factors are not paid their marginal product. Ng (1974) shows that marginal productivity theory is not inconsistent with the possibility of different marginal products in multisectoral models, and Craven (1977) discusses this for models with joint production. Bliss (1975) (see also Dixit, 1977) comes to similar conclusions on the role of marginal products in distribution theory, as we do, but his model is more complex than ours; he concludes that marginal products may put upper and lower limits on wages and prices.

CHAPTER 8

Marxian Theories

We are examining the forces determining the distribution of income in a capitalist economy. There can be no doubt that this is a topic of central importance in the writings of Marx and the Marxists, so that no discussion of distribution theory could be complete without a reference to Marxist thinking. However, the problem that any summary has with Marx and many later writers in the same tradition is that they do not encapsulate their thoughts in a couple of articles in learned journals, or even in a short book. A great number of related economic and social phenomena are bound together in Marxist writing, and we have no hope of doing justice to them all. So, just as we have tried to summarise and simplify the general model of the economy in Chapters 2–6, we must try to extract distribution from a wealth of related topics in Marx. In this chapter we shall meet *labour values* and their use in defining the concept of *exploitation*. We shall not examine Marx's concept of the trade cycle nor the theory that the profit rate tends to decline over time. Both of these require notions of technical progress that we have not yet met.

8.1 LABOUR VALUES

The labour value of a good is defined to be the quantity of labour required in the activity producing it, together with the labour value of the inputs used in its production. In a one-sector model the production of 1 tonne of goods requires the use of b man-weeks of labour, and da tonnes of goods are used up. So, if v is the labour value of 1 tonne of goods,

$$v = b + v(da) \qquad (66)$$

and hence

$$v = \frac{b}{1 - da}$$

105

By comparing this with equation 4 for the price efficiency curve in section 2.1, we see that $v = 1/w(0)$ where $w(0)$ is the real wage when the profit rate is zero.

In the two-sector model the labour value v of a tractor is b plus the labour value of the da tractors used up in production. Again equation 66 holds, and once more $v = b/(1 - da)$. The labour value ϕ of a bushel of corn is the labour β used in the corn activity plus the labour value $v\alpha\delta$ of the tractors used up in the production of a bushel of corn:

$$\phi = \beta + v\alpha\delta$$

since $v = b/(1 - da)$,

$$\phi = \beta + \frac{b\alpha\delta}{1 - da} = \frac{\beta + b\alpha\delta - \beta da}{1 - da}$$

and by comparing this with the equation 13 for the efficiency curve in the two-sector model we see that $\phi = 1/w(0)$.

In an Austrian model, producing corn from labour, the labour needed to produce a bushel of corn is the inverse of the average product of labour. In the example used in section 2.3, $(b_1 + b_2)$ man-weeks of labour produce a bushel of corn, so that the labour value ϕ of corn is equal to $(b_1 + b_2)$, which is equal to $1/w(0)$ from equation 23.

We see that, in all three models, the labour value of one unit of the goods that labourers buy is equal to the inverse of the real wage when $r = 0$. This fact will be particularly useful to us when we make a diagrammatic representation of the Marxian theory.

8.2 THE RATE OF EXPLOITATION

The real wage is given by the efficiency curve $w(r)$ and can therefore be determined when the profit rate has been found by one of the methods of our previous chapters. A labourer can purchase $w(r)$ bushels of corn (we shall use the terminology of the two-sector and Austrian models, but the argument can easily be adapted to be in terms of goods as in the one-sector model), and the labour value of this corn is $\phi w(r)$. Thus from the labour of each man-week employed capitalists receive the product of $[1 - \phi w(r)]$ man-weeks of labour. Since $\phi = 1/w(0)$, and because the efficiency curve slopes down so that $w(0) > w(r)$ when $r > 0$, $[1 - \phi w(r)]$ is positive, and so capitalists receive the product of a positive amount of labour. Capitalists are then said to *exploit* labour because labourers supply more man-weeks of labour than they receive back in the form of goods. The bargain struck between capitalists and labourers sets a money wage, and both sides may think that this is set at a fair level. However, Marxists have argued, even an apparently equitable contract to supply a man-week in return for a money wage w_m masks the true relation between labourers and capitalists, in which the latter can exploit the former because capitalists own not only the capital goods needed for production but also the goods produced. If the labourers owned the capital goods and the outputs, the wage bargain would not be necessary, and all of the national product would be received by labourers.

A useful numerical measure of the inequality of the wage bargain in these Marxist terms is the *rate of exploitation*, e, which is the labour value of the goods received by capitalists divided by the labour value of the goods received by labourers; so

$$e = \frac{1 - \phi w(r)}{\phi w(r)}$$

and since $\phi = 1/w(0)$ we have

$$e = \frac{w(0) - w(r)}{w(r)}$$

The rate of exploitation can be illustrated using the efficiency curve as in Figure 26 where $w(0) = OA$ and $w(r) = OB$ when $r = OC$, so that $e = BA/OB$.

The rate of exploitation is a way of measuring the distribution between labourers and capitalists using not the market value of their receipts but also the labour value of the goods that their incomes allow them to purchase. It is therefore possible to use the rate of exploitation as a statistic of the distribution of income even if we do not wish to make the Marxian interpretation that e measures the inequity of the contract in the labour market, which is masked by the fact that the contract is made in money terms. When

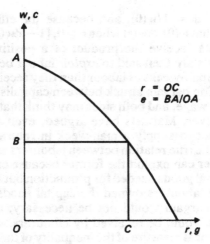

Figure 26 *The rate of exploitation*

we ignore the Marxist interpretation of *e* and view it just as another way of measuring the distribution, *e* conveys the same sort of information as our usual measure of distribution using market prices rk/w.

The use of labour values gives a way of weighting goods that does not involve market prices. It is a method of measurement that would work just as well if all workers were employed by the state and were paid in kind rather than in money. It is then possible that no markets would exist, and so no market prices could be observed for weighting the goods in an aggregate measure such as k or y. In such an economy *e* can be measured using labour values derived from knowledge of the technology, but the calculation of rk/w requires knowledge of the profit rate and of market prices. This example illustrates that labour values are, in a sense, of wider significance than market prices since they can be calculated in a wider variety of economies.

THE TWO MEASURES COMPARED

The two measures of the distribution, rk/w and *e*, are illustrated in Figure 27 where $r = OD$ and $g = OE$, so that $rk/w = GF/OG$. The rate of exploitation is GH/OG, and so in this case $rk/w > e$. If the curve were convex to the origin so that H was above F, the rate of

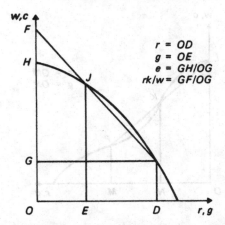

Figure 27   *The distribution and the rate of exploitation*

exploitation would have the greater value. So the relation between the market measure rk/w and the exploitation rate e depends on the shape of the efficiency curve. We can therefore make no general statement that one of the measures must always exceed the other.

The rate of exploitation equals rk/w in three circumstances:

(1)   In a one-sector model, for then the efficiency curve is a straight line. This will also be the case in a two-sector model with equal tractor–labour ratios in the two sectors (see section 2.2).

(2)   By coincidence in a multisectoral model where the efficiency curve may have the shape illustrated in Figure 28. A slight variation in r or g destroys the equality of rk/w and e since KP no longer passes through the intersection of the curve and the w, c axis.

(3)   When the growth rate is zero, for then the points F, H and J in Figure 27 are coincident. In a stationary state the exploitative nature of the wage bargain is as easily described by a price aggregation as by an aggregation using labour values.

The rate of exploitation varies if the profit rate changes; $e = 0$ when $r = 0$, and its maximum level will depend on the level of the subsistence wage that sets a minimum to w. With only one technique available an increase in r reduces the denominator and increases the numerator of the expression for e, so that e must increase. If there is a switch in the chosen technique, $w(0)$ will

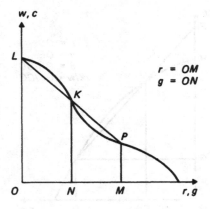

Figure 28

change, and so the rate of exploitation will change as r moves through an intersection of two efficiency curves. As r rises through an intersection e may rise or fall, but it can rise only if there is reswitching between the efficiency curves of two techniques (cf. Figure 20 in section 4.5). The effects of changes in r on e are exactly the same as the effects of changes in r on rk/w when $g = 0$ since the two measures are the same when the growth rate is zero. Hence all of the analysis of changes in rk/w when r varies can be adapted to describe variations in the rate of exploitation.

8.3 THE FUNDAMENTAL THEOREM

The Marxian idea that the contract in the labour market is exploitative against the workers, even though both parties agree to the wage settled, would not be useful if it were possible to show that e could be negative even when capitalists earned positive profits; for if e is negative, $[1 - \phi w(r)]$ must be negative, so that labourers receive a labour value greater than their contribution. This somewhat curious idea is impossible in our simple sorts of models because the efficiency curves slope downwards, and hence $w(r) < w(0)$ whenever r is positive. Morishima (1973) also demonstrates the converse: that whenever r is negative so also is e, thus proving what he calls the *fundamental Marxian theorem* that positive profits and a positive exploitation rate occur in identical circumstances. We are less concerned with the converse because a

110

capitalist system cannot survive if r is negative, since capitalists will consume their capital if there are continued losses in production.

Even though the fundamental Marxian theorem holds in our simple models controversy can arise over the definition of labour values when there are several methods of production available. This controversy becomes more acute when there is beef-and-leather-type joint production as the fundamental theorem can then fail (see Steedman, 1975). However, we shall consider the possibility of alternative techniques as a suitable illustration of the point.

Let us take first the statement that the labour value of a good is equal to the labour time needed in its production; for it may be that, if the economy had to produce only the goods that the workers consumed, a different technique of production would be chosen from that which the profit-maximising capitalists choose. If we seek the technique that produces a bushel of corn with as little labour as possible, we shall know the minimum labour required to produce the workers' purchases. In other words, we seek the technique that produces as much corn as possible per man-week of labour, with no allowance for growth or for capitalists' consumption. We therefore need to find the technique that maximises corn output when the growth rate is zero. Using the quantity interpretation of efficiency curves, we are looking for the technique with the greatest intercept with the c axis. This is technique I in Figure 29

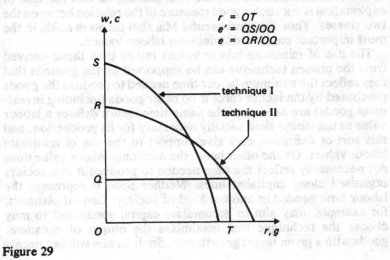

Figure 29

111

where, if $r = OT$, capitalists will choose technique II. The minimum labour time needed to produce a bushel of corn with $g = 0$ (which we shall call the *minimum labour value*) is then the inverse of distance OS, or $1/w_I(0)$. The wage is $w_{II}(r)$ when $r = OT$, and so workers can purchase corn whose minimum labour value is $w_{II}(r)/w_I(0)$. The rate of exploitation e' using minimum labour values is then given by

$$e' = \left(1 - \frac{w_{II}(r)}{w_I(0)} \right) \bigg/ \frac{w_{II}(r)}{w_I(0)}$$

$$= \frac{w_I(0) - w_{II}(r)}{w_{II}(r)}$$

which is QS/OQ in Figure 29. The rate of exploitation e using labour values defined by the chosen technique is QR/OQ, and it is clear that e' can never be less than e. Thus, if r is positive, e will be positive by the fundamental theorem, and so e' will be positive. Morishima (1974) shows that, even in models with joint production where $e < 0$ and $r > 0$ can coexist, it is always true that $r \geqslant g > 0$ implies that $e' > 0$. In the last part of section 3.3 we saw that g can exceed r only if workers save, and then their interest receipts imply that the functional distribution no longer reflects the division of national income between the two classes, so that the rate of exploitation is not such a good measure of the relation between the two classes. Thus the fundamental Marxian theorem holds in the most important cases with minimum labour values.

The use of minimum labour values rather than those derived from the chosen technique can be supported on the grounds that they reflect the minimum labour time needed to produce the goods purchased by the labour force if no other goods (including investment goods) are needed at the same time. Marx defines a labour value as the labour time socially necessary for its production, and this sort of definition may give support to the use of minimum labour values. On the other hand, the minimum labour value does not necessarily reflect the time needed to produce it in a society organised along capitalist lines. Neither need it represent the labour time needed in another kind of society. Central planners, for example, may aim to accumulate capital goods and so may choose the technique that maximises the output of consumer goods with a given target growth rate. Such an aim will not necessarily lead them to choose either the same technique as the capitalists or the technique with the greatest intercept with the c axis. Thus minimum labour values may have little practical significance either in a capitalist economy or in an alternative institutional framework, as they may arise from a technique chosen in neither type of economy.

Marxian theory contains much more than this; we have raised certain questions on the measurement of the distribution using Marxian definitions. These definitions reflect the wage bargain between capitalists and workers, which is a central point in Marx's analysis. Marx himself uses terminology rather different from our own; the labour value of payments to labour and for material used up are referred to as *variable* and *constant capital* respectively, but there is no need to introduce this terminology to capture the flavour of Marxian theory. Writers who have related Marxian theory to current developments in economic theory are referred to in the notes on the literature.

NOTES ON THE LITERATURE

The modern interpretation of Marx is due largely to Morishima (1973). Dobb (1973) places Marx into historical perspective, and Desai (1974) deals with more of the aspects of Marxian thought than we do. The use of minimum labour values stems from Morishima (1974), who calls them optimum values and who seeks to resolve certain problems that arise with joint production pointed out by Steedman (1975). Morishima (1976) and Steedman (1976a) debate the merits of the two definitions of labour values and exploitation. The discussion is carried further in Steedman (1977) and Morishima and Catephores (1978). Craven (1979) discusses the relation between Marxian theory and efficiency curves in models with joint production. Wolfstetter (1973) and von Weizsacker (1973) discuss the proposition that the labour required to expand the capital stock at the same rate as the population should be included in the labour needed to produce the workers' share of the goods. Steedman (1976b) and Wolfstetter (1976) debate this.

CHAPTER 9
Skilled Labour and Land

In this chapter we discuss some topics that generalise our model of the economy without sacrificing too much of the simplicity of the macroeconomic approach to income distribution. We shall introduce, one at a time, some discussion of wage differentials between skilled and unskilled labourers and the rent of land.

The first topic, concerning different types of labour, must be divided into two parts, for the analysis is different according to whether the differences between the two types of labour result from natural distinctions or from training. The most easily recognised natural distinctions are those of sex and age. It may be that a 50-year-old worker is different from a 20-year-old worker purely on grounds of age, even apart from differences of skills brought about through training and experience. We shall call these differences in *primary labour*. Other differences can be induced through training and on-the-job learning. These differences of skill are much more closely allied to produced means of production (like tractors) than to primary inputs (such as basic unskilled labour) and are often said to arise through differences in *human capital*. The decision to invest in the training of a worker may be made in similar circumstances to the decision to invest in a tractor.

We need not devote time to the argument on the extent to which differences in skill are natural or are the product of economic decisions or of environmental factors more generally. This is largely an empirical question, and as with much empirical work there are fundamental questions on causation and on spurious correlation with which we need not concern ourselves here. The reader who objects to the idea that differences in ability are inborn can just ignore the part of the analysis that refers to such distinctions (although he would do well at least to read it to find out its logical structure as it is useful in analysing the rent of land later on).

9.1   DIFFERENCES IN PRIMARY LABOUR

In this section we shall examine the consequences of the existence of two different types of primary labour. We shall use the one-sector model for simplicity of notation and make some remarks on extensions to the two-sector model at the end of the section. We shall also assume for simplicity that the abilities of the two types of labour are mutually exclusive. If they are substitutes (but not perfect substitutes) for each other, several different activities will be available, and each activity will use different amounts of the two types of labour. If type 1 labourers can do the work of type 2 labourers but not vice versa, the supply constraints and conclusions of the model will be somewhat different although the analysis will be of the same form.

Suppose that the production of 1 tonne of goods requires a tonne of goods (which do not depreciate), b man-weeks of type 1 labour and f man-weeks of type 2 labour. If the output of goods is x, then bx and fx man-weeks of the two types will be needed, and it is clear that, except by an unlikely coincidence, the demands for the two types of labour will not both be equal to the given supplies. Economic theory has two possible answers to this: either some of the inputs must be underemployed, or there must be another activity producing goods that uses the inputs in different proportions so that the two activities can be combined to exhaust both supplies.

If one of the types of labour is underemployed, general equilibrium theory tells us that its wage should be zero. This follows from elementary supply and demand analysis since we are saying that, even if the wage is zero, the supply (which we take to be completely inelastic) will exceed the demand, and so the equilibrium wage cannot possibly be above zero. We have already discussed the underemployment of labour in Chapter 6, and we decided there that the minimum reward that can be paid to any labourer is his subsistence. Let us therefore suppose that type 2 labour is paid a subsistence real wage $\bar{w}_2$. The price equation is then

$$1 = ra + w_1 b + \bar{w}_2 f$$

and so the efficiency curve relating w_1 to r and $\bar{w}_2$ is

$$w_1 = \frac{1 - ra - \bar{w}_2 f}{b}$$

When $w_2 = 0$ we have the equation for the price efficiency curve in the one-sector model (cf. equation 4); and so, as we should expect, the effect of a positive wage for the second type of labour is to shift the curve relating w_1 to r towards the origin.

Since the second type of labour is paid only a subsistence wage, all of that wage will be spent on consumption. So, if the stock of goods used (ax) grows at rate g, the consumption output per man-week of type 1 labour (c) that is available to type 1 labourers and to capitalists will be given by

$$cbx = x - gax - \bar{w}_2 fx$$

and so

$$c = \frac{1 - ga - \bar{w}_2 f}{b}$$

Hence, the quantity efficiency curve has exactly the same form as the price efficiency curve derived above. The national accounting indentities are (per man-week of type 1)

$$y \equiv rk + w_1 + \frac{\bar{w}_2 fx}{bx}$$

$$y \equiv gk + c + \frac{\bar{w}_2 fx}{bx}$$

and so the value of capital per man-week of type 1 is given by the slope of the efficiency curve exactly as in the one-sector model of section 2.1:

$$k = \frac{c - w_1}{r - g}$$

The distribution is illustrated in Figure 30, which is different from the standard diagrams of Chapter 3 only in that the additional distance OA $(= BC)$ is now included to represent the wage paid to type 2 labour (per man-week of type 1 labour).

Let us now suppose that both kinds of labour are fully employed and that this is achieved through the use of two activities for the production of goods. One tonne of goods can be produced either by b and f man-weeks working with a non-depreciating goods, or by

116

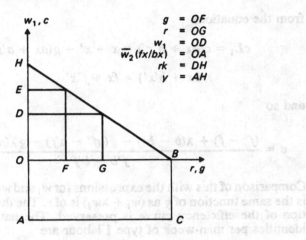

Figure 30 *Distribution with two types of labour*

b' and f' man-weeks working with a' of the same kind of goods. The two price equations are

$$1 = ra + w_1 b + w_2 f$$

$$1 = ra' + w_1 b' + w_2 f'$$

These equations can be solved to give w_1 and w_2 as functions of r:

$$w_1 = \frac{(f' - f) - r(af' - a'f)}{f'b - b'f}$$

$$w_2 = \frac{(b - b') - r(a'b - ab')}{f'b - b'f}$$

The sum of wage payments per man-week of type 1 can then be obtained as a function of r. If the supplies of the two types of labour are L_1 and L_2, the sum of labour payments per man-week of type 1 labour will be $(w_1 + \lambda w_2)$ where $\lambda = L_2/L_1$.

If the outputs of the two activities are x and x', the stock of goods used in production will be $(ax + a'x')$. If this stock grows at rate g, consumption output per man-week of type 1 labour can be found

117

from the equations

$$cL_1 = c(bx + b'x') = x + x' - g(ax + a'x')$$

$$\lambda(bx + b'x') = fx + f'x'$$

and so

$$c = \frac{(f' - f) + \lambda(b - b') - g(af' - a'f) - g\lambda(a'b - ab')}{f'b - b'f}$$

Comparison of this with the expressions for w_1 and w_2 shows that c is the same function of g as $(w_1 + \lambda w_2)$ is of r. The dual interpretation of the efficiency curve is preserved. The national income identities per man-week of type 1 labour are

$$y = rk + w_1 + w_2\lambda$$

$$y = gk + c$$

so that

$$k = \frac{c - w_1 - w_2\lambda}{r - g}$$

The usual efficiency curve diagram then shows the distribution between profits and the sum of wage payments to both types of labour.

CHOICE OF TECHNIQUE

The two different kinds of outcome described above are in effect different techniques of production. To illustrate the choice between these techniques consider an example in which there are two activities for producing goods: activity 1 uses 1 tonne of goods, two man-weeks of type 1 labour and three man-weeks of type 2 labour to produce 1 tonne of goods; activity 2 uses 4 tonnes of goods, two man-weeks of type 1 and one man-week of type 2. We suppose that for every four man-weeks of type 1 there are three man-weeks of type 2 available, so that $\lambda = 3/4$, and that the subsistence minimum wage is 1/8. There are in principle twelve

118

possible techniques as shown in Table 6. It is, however, not possible to use activity 1 with type 1 labour fully employed since activity 1 requires three man-weeks of type 2 for every man-week of type 1, and so the demand for type 2 labour would exceed the supply. Similarly, we cannot use activity 2 and fully employ type 2 labour. Neither activity uses the types of labour in the same proportions as they are supplied, so that neither activity can be used alone if both types of labour are to be fully employed. If both activities are used, and only type 1 labour is fully employed, w_2 will be at subsistence. Hence, in order to earn the same profit rate r that is consistent with the use of both activities the wage w_1 and the profit rate r must satisfy

$$1 = r + 2w_1 + {}^3/_8$$
$$1 = 4r + 2w_1 + {}^1/_8$$

| | Activities used | | |
	1	2	Both
Labour	1	no	II $r = 1/12$
types	2	I	no $r = 3/22$
fully	Both	no	no III
employed	Neither	$r = 3/8$	no	no

Table 6 *Possible techniques*

so that $r = 1/12$ and $w_1 = 13/48$. Similarly, it can be shown that the only profit rate that is consistent with the use of both activities and w_1 at subsistence is $r = 3/22$. Finally, if neither type of labour is fully employed, labour costs in the two activities will be 5/8 and 3/8 respectively, and so the profit rates will be 3/8 in activity 1 and 5/32 in activity 2. Thus if neither type is fully employed, the profit rate must be 3/8 and activity 1 will be chosen. So, unless the profit rate happens to be 1/12, 3/22 or 3/8 one of the techniques labelled I, II and III in Table 6 must be used.

When $r = 0$ activity 2 must be used since it has lower wage costs whatever the real wage. Thus technique II must be chosen, $w_1 = 7/16$ and $w_2 = 1/8$. When $r = 1/8$ technique I gives $w_1 = 1/8$ and $w_2 = 5/24$, but with these wages labour costs in activity 2 are $[2(1/8) + 5/24]$, which equals 11/24, leaving a profit of 13/24 and hence a profit rate on the 4 tonnes of goods used of 13/96, which is greater than 1/8. Hence technique I cannot be chosen since the activity not included in it yields a greater profit and the capitalists would switch to it. Similarly, if technique II is used, $w_1 = 3/16$ and $w_2 = 1/8$, and these wages give labour costs in activity 1 of $[2(3/16) + 3(1/8)]$, which equals $3/4$, so that the profit rate in activity 1 is $1/4$. Thus, profit maximisers will not use technique II since it gives rise to prices that tempt them to switch to the other activity. Hence, technique III will be used, and w_1 and w_2 are simultaneously determined from the two price equations

$$1 = \frac{1}{8} + 2w_1 + 3w_2$$

$$1 = \frac{1}{2} + 2w_1 + w_2$$

so that $w_1 = 5/32$ and $w_2 = 3/16$. Finally, when $r = 9/64$ technique I yields $w_1 = 1/8$ and $w_2 = 13/64$, and these give labour costs of $29/64$ in activity 2 and hence a profit rate of $35/256$ in that activity. This profit rate is less than $9/64$, so that profit maximisers are not tempted to switch to activity 2. Thus, technique I can be chosen. It can be shown that technique II cannot be chosen by profit maximisers and that technique III gives rise to a real wage below subsistence.

The example illustrates that the possibilities for the full employment of each type of labour depend on the profit rate. We have not discussed the forces determining the profit rate and the growth rate, but there is no difficulty in introducing the equality of savings and investment to provide a link between r and g. We saw in section 5.4 that if the distribution is not changing from week to week the savings of wage earners will be irrelevant to the relation between r and g, and this conclusion is completely unaffected by the introduction of more than one type of labour; for the capitalists save $s_c r(k - z)$ where z is now the sum of interest payments to both types of labour per man-week of type 1 labour, and these savings are used to increase the capitalists' own resources $(k - z)$ at rate g, so that $s_c r = g$.

The question of full employment is rather more tricky since in Chapter 6 we discussed how we could close the model by assuming that a steadily growing labour force was fully employed, but now we can only close the model in this way if the two different types of labour increase in supply at the same rate. Otherwise, there will eventually be a bottleneck in production, and some of the more abundant type of labour will need to be left idle. The assumption of equal growth rates for the two supplies may not be unreasonable if they are merely two parts of a steadily growing population, such as male and female labour or 'young' and 'old' labour in a society whose population has grown at the same rate for many weeks. Only in this sort of circumstance can technique III be used over a large number of weeks.

THE TWO-SECTOR MODEL

The analysis in the two-sector model is very similar to that in the one-sector case, except that the algebra is more difficult. The price equations for each sector now need to include wage payments to both types of labour, and once again there are two types of solution possible. One of the types of labour may not be fully employed and hence may be paid a subsistence wage. Then one activity is used in each sector; and if, for example, w_2 is at subsistence, the two price equations will determine w_1 and the price ratio p / π in terms of r. Alternatively, both types of labour may be fully employed with wages above subsistence, and a second activity may be used in one or other of the sectors. Then there are three price equations to determine the two real wages and the price ratio in terms of r. On the quantity side the output levels of the three activities are chosen so that the supplies and demands of the two types of labour and of the tractors used are equal. The wage differential between the two types of labour, and the employment prospects for each type, are again dependent on the profit rate.

9.2 TRAINING AND HUMAN CAPITAL

Wage differentials also arise from the acquisition of skills by some of the labour force. To analyse the results of such education we shall assume that all labourers are born with the same basic abilities, so that the problem of differentials derived from natural distinctions does not arise. Some of this unskilled labour force becomes skilled through education, and this education is an activity of production requiring the labour of teachers to convert an input of unskilled labour into an output of skilled labour. The process of education may also require other inputs, and so let us take our previous two-sector model and extend it to include an education sector. We shall assume that an input of A non-depreciating tractors and M man-weeks of skilled labour (in the form of teachers) can be used to convert one unskilled labourer into a skilled labourer. We shall assume that this activity takes one week to complete. Further, to avoid the complication of having more than one type of skilled labour in the model (this can be included with sufficient algebraic labour) we shall assume that skilled labourers, like university teachers, are able to teach others as soon as their own training is ended.

The process of education produces a capital asset: a skill whose owners expect to receive a wage higher than that of their unskilled counterparts. If education is run privately, the profit rate in the education sector will be the same as that in other sectors as capitalists will choose between establishing schools, tractor factories and corn farms according to profitability. By a simple extension of the analysis of Chapter 2, factories, schools and farms can coexist only if they achieve the same profit rate. If students are willing to pay a price P for their education, that price must cover the wages of teachers and profit on the A tractors needed to educate the student. If the wages of skilled and unskilled labourers are w_s and w_u respectively and if the profit rate is r, the price equation for the operation of schools will be

$$P = rpA + w_2M \qquad (67)$$

Assuming that students purchase their education solely for the benefit of receiving a future wage differential $(w_s - w_u)$, they will only become educated if the rate of return to their investment in training is no lower than the rate of return to an investment in tractors. If the return to education is higher than that to tractors, the demand for education will rise and that for tractors will fall, and the only possible equilibrium will be where the two rates of return are the same. So, in the simplest case where labourers are assumed to live for ever, the wage differential $(w_s - w_u)$ must equal r times the cost of an education, which is the price P paid for it plus the unskilled wage w_u foregone during the week at school. Thus

$$w_s - w_u = r(P + w_u) \qquad (68)$$

just as the return to the owner of an everlasting tractor is rp. If we allow for human mortality and assume that the differential between w_s and w_u can be earned for T weeks after the end of training, the discounted stream of future wage differentials must be equal to the cost of the education:

$$P + w_u = \frac{w_s - w_u}{1 + r} + \frac{w_s - w_u}{(1 + r)^2} + \ldots + \frac{w_s - w_u}{(1 + r)^T} \quad (69)$$

so that

$$w_s - w_u = R(P + w_u) \quad (70)$$

where from equation 69

$$R = \frac{r}{1 - \dfrac{1}{(1 + r)^T}} \quad (71)$$

We shall develop our analysis using equation 70 rather than equation 68, but it is clear that for any r the two equations are very similar when T is large since $1/(1 + r)^T$ is then very close to zero and R is very close to r. The use of equation 70 rather than equation 68 can also allow for the possibility that students may regard education as both current consumption and as an investment, so that they are prepared to earn a lower rate of return on their investment in education than on investment in tractors. R will then be less than the equation 71 indicates (or greater if students hate school so much that they demand a higher rate of return), but all of our subsequent analysis will be unchanged.

The two remaining sectors, producing tractors and corn, have conventional price equations. If one tractor is produced by b unskilled and m skilled man-weeks of labour working with a tractors, and if one bushel of corn is produced by β man-weeks of unskilled labour (and no skilled labour to simplify the algebra) working with α tractors, the price equations in the tractor and corn sectors will be

$$\frac{p}{\pi} = r\frac{p}{\pi}a + w_u b + w_s m$$

$$1 = r\frac{p}{\pi}\alpha + w_u \beta$$

These can be used in conjunction with equations 67 and 70 to give expressions for w_u and w_s in terms of r and R, which is itself a function of r according to equation 71:

123

$$w_u = \frac{(1-ra)(1-RM)-RrAm}{\beta[(1-ra)(1-RM)-rRAm]+r\alpha[(1+R)m+b(1-RM)]}$$

$$w_s = \frac{(1-ra)(1-RM)-RrAm}{\beta[(1-ra)(1-RM)-rRAm]+r\alpha[(1+R)m+b(1-RM)]}$$

If the supplies of tractors and of skilled labour are s and S and the outputs of corn, tractors and skilled labour are ξ, x and X respectively, the supplies of and demands for tractors and skilled labour will be equal when

$$ax + AX + \alpha\xi = s$$

$$mx + MX = S$$

Of the labour force L, $(b + m)x$ are employed in the tractor sector and $\beta\xi$ in the corn sector. In the education sector MX are working as teachers and X are students, so that

$$(b + m)x + \beta\xi + (1 + M)X = L$$

Then if the stocks of tractors and of skills grow at rates g and G so that $x = gs$ and $X = GS$, we can derive an expression for consumption output per man-week of the labour force (skilled and unskilled together):

$$c = \frac{\xi}{L} = \frac{(1 - ga)(1 - GM) - GgAm}{\beta[(1 - ga)(1 - GM) - gGAm] + g\alpha[(1 + G)m + b(1 - GM)]}$$

Comparison of the expressions for w_u and for c tells us that the unskilled wage is related to r and R in the same way as c is related to g and G. In addition, if the amount of skilled labour grows at the same rate as the tractor stock – as, for example, must occur if a steadily growing labour force is to be fully employed over a long period – and if equation 71 holds, G will be the same function of g as R is of r, for the output X of skilled labour must be sufficient for the stock S to grow at rate g and to replace those skilled labourers who leave the work force after T weeks. These will be the workers who trained T weeks ago; and since the number of skilled workers

124

is growing at rate g, there will be $X/(1+g)^T$ who finished training T weeks ago. Hence

$$X = GS = gS + \frac{X}{(1+g)^T}$$

so that

$$G = \frac{g}{1 - \frac{1}{(1+g)^T}}$$

which is of exactly the same form as equation 71.

The national accounts must now contain the returns to, and the accumulation of, skill. The number of skilled labourers is S, and the price paid to become skilled is $(P + w_u)$ so that the total value of skills is $(P + w_u)S$. We shall define h to be the value of skills per man-week of the labour force, so that

$$h = \frac{(P + w_u)S}{L}$$

and if the stock of skill is growing at the same rate as the tractor stock, the identities (expressed net of the production of skill needed to offset retirements) will be

$$y = rk + w_u + rh$$

$$y = gk + c + gh$$

The expression $(c - w_u)/(r - g)$ now measures the sum of the values of *physical capital* (tractors) and *human capital* (skills), and our usual distribution diagram tells us the distribution between wages and profits on human and non-human capital taken together. Each skilled labourer receives an unskilled wage w_u plus an additional payment that is the return to his human capital. The functional distribution $r(k + h)/w_u$ now measures the distribution between produced inputs (tractors and skills) and primary inputs (labour before training) rather than between labour and capital.

125

9.3 THE RENT OF LAND

The methods used above to analyse wage differentials can be applied in a variety of other circumstances. Our two approaches have demonstrated the way to include either an additional primary factor or an additional produced input. In the latter case there is very little difference between a model with two types of machines and a model in which tractors and educated labour are the two inputs produced. The analysis of the rent of land is closely related to our discussion of wage differences that arise from natural variations in the labour force. Land has traditionally been regarded as a primary input not produced in the economy, although Johnson (1973) argues that land should be regarded as a produced factor of production, akin to tractors rather than labour. He argues that, if the return to land is high, reclamation of unused land will go on until the cost of reclaiming another hectare rises to such an extent that capitalists are indifferent between producing tractors and reclaiming land. The decision whether to treat land as though it is a primary input or as a producible good depends largely on the scope for reclamation and the time involved in that operation; for if little or no land can be produced, or if the time is very long, we may treat land as being in fixed supply for a considerable period, so that a model in which land is treated as a primary input may be a closer approximation to reality than one in which land is an output from a process of production. It should be noted here that we are not concerned with technical progress that increases the output from a hectare of land through improvements in farming technology. We are concerned with a fixed technology that requires the use of land in some given proportions to other inputs.

To develop a theory of the rent of land that is a primary input we can reinterpret the input requirements f and f' used in section 9.1 as inputs of land. Then w_2 is the rent of land and λ is the ratio of the fixed supply of land (measured in hectares) to the fixed supply of labour (now assumed to be all of one type). The efficiency curve relates the sum of payments to providers of primary factors ($w_1 + \lambda w_2$) to the profit rate. If some land is left idle, all land will have a zero rent since any attempt to charge for its use can be countered by moving to some unused area. The analysis of section 9.1 can therefore be simplified in so far as we can disregard the subsistence requirement for land. The numerical example used in section 9.1 can be interpreted to tell us that the wage of labour, the rent of land

126

and the possibility of underemployment of the primary factors all depend on the profit rate.

DIFFERENTIAL RENT

The only remaining concept usually associated with the use of land is that of differential rent. Like wage differentials that arise when some have different skills from others, differential rent arises when some areas of land are of different qualities from others. The theory appears at its simplest when the same input of tractors and labour produces more in one area of land than in another. Suppose that there are three types of land in use, which produce respectively three, two and one bushel of corn per hectare when β man-weeks work with α tractors. The rents q_1, q_2 and q_3 of the three types will be related in the three price equations

$$3\pi = q_1 + r\alpha p + w_m\beta \tag{72}$$

$$2\pi = q_2 + r\alpha p + w_m\beta \tag{73}$$

$$\pi = q_3 + r\alpha p + w_m\beta \tag{74}$$

and we shall have also a price equation in the tractor sector (where we assume for simplicity that no land is needed)

$$p = rpa + w_m b$$

These four equations contain five variables: w_m/π, p/π, q_1/π, q_2/π and q_3/π, which we want to express as functions of the profit rate, so that they can all be determined when the profit rate is known. A fifth equation can be added by assuming either that the supply of the worst quality land is not used up, so that $q_3 = 0$, or by assuming that some other activity is also used in one or other of the sectors, just as we needed to assume that two activities were used in the one-sector model to use up the supplies of two types of labour. Which ever way we add the fifth equation, equations 72–74 imply that $q_1 = q_3 + 2$ and $q_2 = q_3 + 1$, so that each type of land generates an income that exceeds q_3 by the amount of its greater productivity.

A more complicated case arises if the different types of land require different ratios of labour to tractors to produce a bushel of corn; for if land of type i has rent q_i and requires β_i labour working with α_i tractors to produce a bushel of corn, the price equations will be

$$1 = q_i + r\alpha_i p + w\beta_i$$

for each i. Then, even if some land is left idle so that one of the $q_i = 0$, it may not be possible to identify the free land until the profit rate is known. Intuitively, if tractors are cheap and labour is expensive, the free land will be likely to be the one that needs many man-weeks per tractor since it will be expensive to use that sort of activity. Conversely, if a change in the profit rate makes tractors more expensive and labour cheaper, a type of land requiring many tractors per man-week will not be in demand and so will be free. An example similar to that used in section 9.1 can be employed to show the relation between the profit rate and the differential rents of lands having different input requirements. It is only in the simple case where α_i/β_i is the same for all the land that we can name the 'best' and 'worst' land from the capitalists' point of view without knowing the profit rate.

NOTES ON THE LITERATURE

The use of more than one primary factor has been discussed by Sraffa (1960), but much of the literature on distribution and capital theory has ignored the problem. The human capital approach to wage differentials is well established: see Blaug (1970), Becker (1975), Mincer (1958), Oulton (1974) and readings in Blaug (1968). Differential rents on lands of different fertility is a concept of Ricardo (1817). See also Pasinetti (1960).

CHAPTER 10
Uncertainty

Although our previous chapter introduced incomes other than wages and profits we have not modified the basic theory of the functional distribution between those who provide primary factors and those who own some produced asset. In this chapter we shall examine the extent to which we need to alter the model to account for the fact that some future events can be predicted only with a considerable degree of uncertainty. We shall ask whether there is a function performed by some members of the economy who take on risky ventures and receive a part of national income for doing so.

10.1 ENTREPRENEURIAL INCOME

We shall define an *entrepreneur* as someone who employs labour, rents machinery (or borrows the money to buy it) from capitalists and organises these inputs in activities of production. At the start of the week he contracts to pay wages and rentals for the machines (or interest on his borrowings), and it is he who takes the risk that at the end of the week the revenue may not be sufficient to make these contracted payments. It is he also who receives the surplus if the revenue exceeds the contracted payments. We shall call this difference between revenue and contracted costs *entrepreneurial income*; it may, of course, be either positive or negative, and in the latter case the entrepreneur must himself make up the difference. Knight (1921), who is principally associated with theories of this kind, refers to this entrepreneurial income as profit and to the income of those who own the capital goods (or lend out the money to buy them) as interest. To avoid confusion with our earlier chapters we shall refer to the latter as profit.

Entrepreneurial income arises as a result of uncertainty. If the outcome of all activities were known with certainty, the capitalists could employ wage-earning managers to organise production, and these managers would receive a contracted wage. There would be

129

no residue between revenue and contracted payments where the latter include profit at the normal rate r. When there is uncertainty someone must bear the risk, and so entrepreneurial income has a place in functional distribution theory. It should be noted that some individuals may receive income both as entrepreneurs and as capitalists, since property owners may take an active part in running activities or may lend out their assets on an equity basis, receiving more from successful than from unsuccessful companies. Furthermore, if contracts are not fulfilled when an entrepreneur is bankrupt, some of the risks will be borne by wage earners and those who lend capital goods. They will demand a share of entrepreneurial income in return for taking these risks. Thus, those who work for or lend to risky companies will contract for higher incomes than those who deal with safer ventures. However, the fact that an element of a wage earner's income may be due to the risks that he takes that his employer will not fulfil the contract does not detract from the difference of function between suppliers of labour and takers of risks. Similarly, the existence of equity finance should not blur the distinction between capitalists' profits and entrepreneurial income. Wages and profits will exist without uncertainty; entrepreneurial income will not.

Entrepreneurial income may be positive or negative, and without any further analysis we may suspect that on average the negative and the positive cancel out. In the next section we shall see whether there is any *a priori* reason to suppose that aggregate entrepreneurial income is positive by looking at the microeconomics of decision taking under uncertainty. We shall then incorporate the results of this analysis into the theory of earlier chapters.

10.2 INDIVIDUAL BEHAVIOUR UNDER UNCERTAINTY

The formal analysis of individual choices when outcomes are uncertain proceeds through the definition of a *certainty equivalent*. An individual is asked to evaluate the prospect of a project with an uncertain outcome in comparison with a guaranteed income. If the individual is indifferent between the prospect of receiving X with certainty and some uncertain project, the certainty equivalent of that uncertain project for that individual is X. The individual can then compare several uncertain projects by ranking their uncertainty equivalents. It may be that a certainty equivalent for an uncertain project can be found from a possible course of action that is open to the individual. For example, the owner of a machine may be able to make a contract to rent out his machine for a fixed profit, or he may be able to act as entrepreneur himself and receive an uncertain income. If he is indifferent between the fixed contract and the prospect of becoming an entrepreneur, the profit that he can receive by contract will be the uncertainty equivalent of the entrepreneurial venture. If no such choice is open, the individual must answer a hypothetical question to find his certainty equivalents.

If we assume in addition that individuals can associate a probability of occurrence with each possible outcome of an uncertain project, that project has a calculable *expected value*. This expected value is the sum of the incomes in the various situations multiplied by the probabilities that those situations will occur. If there are three possible outcomes that give rise to incomes X_1, X_2 and X_3 with probabilities π_1, π_2 and π_3, the expected value of the project will be $\pi_1 X_1 + \pi_2 X_2 + \pi_3 X_3$. We shall say that the individual is *risk averse* if the certainty equivalent of a project is less than its expected value; for then, if a project is available that yields a certain outcome that is just greater than the certainty equivalent of the uncertain project but below its expected value, he will prefer the certain project even though on average the uncertain project yields a greater return. Thus, he is willing to sacrifice a higher average return that is uncertain for a lower, but certain, return. For example, suppose that an entrepreneur makes contracts to pay wages and profits of £100. He believes that there is a probability of 0·05 that his factory will burn down and hence that he will receive no revenue; his loss will then be £100. There is a probability of 0·95 that he will receive a revenue of £120 and hence an entrepreneurial income of £20. The expected value of this project to the entrepreneur is (0·05) (−£100) + (0·95) (£20) = £14. If the certainty equivalent is, say, £12, the individual will be risk averse. He will be willing to pay an insurance premium of, say, £7 to guarantee that his revenue will be £120 whether or not a fire occurs, for then his contractual payments will be £107 and he will have a certain income of £13, which he prefers to the uncertain project even though the expected value of the latter is greater. We notice that, if this entrepreneur's view of the probabilities is borne out by the experience of many others in similar positions, the insurance company will not on average make a loss, for out of every 100 such projects that it insures for an income of £700 it will pay out on average to only five, at a cost of £600. Assuming that the outbreak of fire in one factory is independent of its outbreak in another, the insurance company can pool the uncertainties so that there is a very high probability that it will not make a loss.

When insurance is available the entrepreneur ceases to have the risk-taking function defined above, and so, except as a manager receiving a wage, the capitalists have no need of him. The entrepreneurial function and income are transferred to the insurance company, and in the sort of example that we have constructed it is clear that the entrepreneurial income is positive. Some income, on average positive, can therefore be attributed to the fact that the projects are uncertain. If there were no uncertainty, the insurance companies would not exist, and there would be no entrepreneurial income. The capitalists would be as well off with a certainty equivalent that was less than the average uncertain return, and so a lower national income would give rise to the same level of well-being. The fact that entrepreneurial income is on average positive in an uncertain economy of risk-averse individuals hides the fact that some individuals (and even some insurance companies) will receive a negative income in some weeks. These individuals need to make up the deficit from their own resources, but over several weeks they should expect to recoup more than they have lost.

An opposite analysis can be carried out if an individual displays *risk preference*. This is the case if the certainty equivalent of the project exceeds its expected value. If in our example above the certainty equivalent is £16 rather than £12, the entrepreneur will not be willing to pay an insurance premium of more than £4 to guarantee his revenue of £120; for if the premium is, say, £5, his contracted payments will be £105 and his guaranteed income will be £15, which is less than his certainty equivalent. The insurance company is likely to make a loss if it receives only £4 from each of 100 clients, as its payments will on average be £600 with an income of £400. The existence of gambling, where average prizes are less than the average stake, indicates that some people sometimes express risk preference, but Green (1971, pp. 233–9), who studies the theory of choice under uncertainty in greater depth, claims that risk aversion is more relevant to 'wealth oriented' activities (including entrepreneurial behaviour) than is any form of risk preference. In so far as Green is correct in that view, entrepreneurial income is positive on average.

10.3 INVESTMENT AND SAVING: A KEYNESIAN THEORY

The main role of uncertainty in our model is to enable us to make a convincing divorce between decisions to save and decisions to invest. We touched briefly on this in section 5.7; but where there was no uncertainty entrepreneurs had no function, and the savings propensity of capitalists reflected also their desire to buy machines for use in production. Thus, their decision to save was at the same time a decision to invest.

The microeconomic analysis of the last section gives a particular function to entrepreneurs who decide the level of resources to be used in each sector. In particular they decide on how many capital goods are to be produced (or at least they aim at an expected number; the actual production may be one of the uncertainties of the model) on the basis of the wage and capital costs that they face and their own entrepreneurial income. We shall assume that the entrepreneurs are risk averse and that they receive the difference between the actual outcome and the certainty equivalent. Thus contracted payments are equal to the certainty equivalent of the projects. It is simplest to assume that the entrepreneurs spend all of their incomes on consumption goods (after the negative incomes have been covered by those with positive incomes), since otherwise they could use their savings to become capitalists in their own right, and the distinction between savings and investment decisions would again become blurred.

The distinction between saving and investment decisions is one of the features of Keynesian macroeconomic theory, and it permits us to develop a Keynesian theory of income distribution. In such a theory the supply of money determines the rate of return to *bonds* via the liquidity preference of individuals. This is a standard argument, which can be found in macreconomic texts (and, of course, in Keynes, 1936), and so we shall not develop the argument here. For our purposes the principal feature of bonds is that they are assets whose weekly return is known with certainty. So, as far as capitalists are concerned an agreement to lend their assets to an entrepreneur for a fixed return is equivalent to the purchase of a bond. Hence, the profit rate received by capitalists is equal to the rate of return on bonds. Thus, r is determined by the supply of money and liquidity preference. In consequence we know which technique must be chosen, and we know the real wage and the relative prices of goods.

133

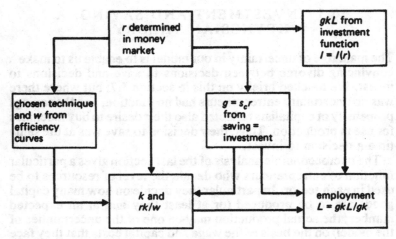

Figure 31 *Structure of the Keynesian model*

The next stage of the argument, illustrated in Figure 31, follows Chapter 5; for even though saving and investment decisions are made by different groups, total savings and total investment must be equal. Hence, an equation such as $g = s_c r$ can be used to determine the growth rate. We can then derive the distribution of income in the usual way and also determine the value of capital per man-week employed and the level of investment per man-week employed gk.

We have therefore determined the functional distribution from the money market and the equality of savings and investment, but we can extract some more information by using the fact that separate individuals are making decisions to save and to invest. Entrepreneurs will decide the level of investment on the basis of the costs and revenues that they expect to have. Their decisions therefore depend on the profit rate, the wage and the prices of the goods. The wage and prices depend on the profit rate, so that the amount of investment I is a function of the profit rate. When there is only one investment good we can distinguish between the quality of investment and its price, but even in more complicated cases both the prices and the quantities decided by entrepreneurs depend on the profit rate. The usual intuitive argument is that total investment will be reduced if the profit rate paid to capitalists (which is called the interest rate in many analyses of Keynes) is increased. The argument is that, if r increases, there will be fewer projects that can yield a sufficient entrepreneurial income above contracted payments, but since the wage and prices also change when r changes it is possible that contracted payments may *fall* as r rises and so make investment more attractive.

The possibility of counterintuitive movements in I does not alter the fact that the profit rate determines the level of investment via entrepreneurial decisions. This total level of investment is the growth in the capital stock gK (we ignore depreciation for simplicity), and this in turn is equal to gK multiplied by the number of man-weeks of labour employed. We have already determined gk from the money market and the savings propensities, and so the only variable remaining to be determined from investment behaviour is the level of employment L. This is found by dividing total investment I by gk. The endogenous determination of the level of employment is a Keynesian feature that we have been able to add to the model now that we can make a convincing separation between decisions to save and decisions to invest.

In a more general model in which 'everything depends on everything else', the apparent causal chain linking the money market to the distribution and to the level of employment needs to be replaced by a simultaneous system in which all of the markets and decisions may interact. The return to bonds could not then be determined without reference to individual demands and supplies for bonds and capital goods as is the case in the simpler Keynesian model. The simultaneous system would enable us to iron out some of the problems of the Keynesian analysis, including the fact that the level of investment, the real wage and the profit rate are inter-related in a more complex way than our analysis suggests. This is because the average level of entrepreneurial income will depend on the amount of resources used in production in each sector; and since the entrepreneurs take their share of the national product, the size of their incomes must affect the real incomes of wage earners and capitalists. Thus, the efficiency curve and the national accounts need to be adapted to include entrepreneurial income. These complications will limit the explanatory power of our theory, and it is worth making the simplifications of our Keynesian theory in order to see how different parts of the economy interact. Even in a more complicated model, decisions to save, to invest and to hold money will be crucial in determining the distribution and the level of employment.

The Keynesian introduction of a separate investment function and a money market to determine r removes the necessity to use either the full employment or the fixwage condition of Chapter 6. Full employment is possible in the Keynesian model if the model supply can be manipulated in such a way that the profit rate determines L equal to the labour supply. This may not be an easy task given that L depends on both the investment function and the shape of the efficiency curve (used to determine k), so that the effects of changes in r are not even of unambiguous direction, let alone size. Fiscal policy that increases I without changes in r may be more effective, but even this may have other effects on the model if the extra investment is financed through the money market.

We now have several possible ways of closing our model of distribution. The full employment, fixwage and Keynesian theories all make use of the form of the technology (via efficiency curves) and the savings behaviour of individuals, but they differ in the final assumptions needed to close the model. The Keynesian and full employment theories also fix the level of employment, and a fixwage theory could do so if it were combined with a separate investment function. The argument is then exactly as in the Keynesian model except that the fixwage replaces the effect of the money market in determining r (and hence w). This is as far as we shall take our macroeconomic models of distribution with a fixed technology. Our final task is to see how technical progress enters into distribution theory.

NOTES ON THE LITERATURE

Individual behaviour under uncertainty has been treated in depth by Green (1971) and also by Baumol (1961). The classic writing on the role of uncertainty in distribution theory is Knight (1921), although, as discussed in section 10.1, his terminology differs from ours. Basic Keynesian employment theory (Keynes, 1936) has been expounded in a multitude of macroeconomics texts.

CHAPTER 11
Technical Progress: Introduction

In the preceding chapters we have analysed models in which an increase in real wages can occur only if the profit rate and the level of profits per man-week are reduced. In Chapter 3 we demonstrated this in the two-sector model with a single technique, and in Chapter 8 we showed the same result when the distribution is measured in Marxian terms as the rate of exploitation. With several techniques it is possible to increase rk whilst keeping w constant at an intersection between two efficiency curves, but we have not so far analysed any model of the economy that can provide a continuing increase in both the real wage and the level of profits per man-week. Similarly, we have not found any way of increasing consumption per man-week without reducing investment.

The only form of sustained growth in the economy that we have so far been able to analyse is that which results from increases in employment. This does not allow increases in output and income per man-week. We shall now turn to examine the possibility that output can also grow through increases in productivity. We shall refer to all such increases in the productive potential of the economy as *technical progress*.

In the first and second sections of this chapter we shall examine ways in which technical progress can arise in practice. Later in the chapter we shall show how technical progress affects the efficiency curve, and we shall identify some kinds of neutral progress in which the efficiency curve shifts in some simple way. These definitions of neutral progress are useful for classifying technical progress into 'labour saving' and 'capital saving' types. They are also of considerable theoretical importance, as we shall see in the next chapter where we shall discuss the effect of technical progress on the distribution and the converse influence of the costs of inputs on the form of technical progress that the capitalists choose to implement.

The introduction of technical progress complicates our models, and so much of our discussion takes place in the one-sector model. We have learned by now that this has the disadvantage of ignoring the possibility of changes in the structure of production and changes in relative prices. In Chapter 13 we shall introduce technical progress to the two-sector model and discuss some of the difficulties that arise. However, we shall not develop the model to its fullest extent as this requires considerable algebra but does not really produce much greater insight into the workings of the economy.

In all our discussions of technical progress we shall ignore uncertainty and the complications of skilled labour and land. This will enable us to see the influence of progress more clearly, although it is undoubtedly true that the possibility of technical advance is one of the major sources of uncertainty and that the introduction of risky new technology is one of the main functions of the entrepreneur. Furthermore, changes in the skills of the labour force are one of the results of technical progress. Thus, our neglect of uncertainty and skilled labour to concentrate on progress is not an end in itself; the tools that we shall develop in these three chapters need to be combined with those of the last two to give a clearer picture of the workings of the economy. This complicated task is beyond the scope of this book.

11.1 TYPES OF TECHNICAL PROGRESS

Technical progress manifests itself in many ways in practice. First, a new way of combining the inputs in an activity may be developed. This is the simplest form of technical progress in the sense that no new good is involved; its effect is simply to change one or more of the input coefficients. We shall return to its effects on efficiency curves in section 11.3 below.

A second form of technical progress involves the introduction of new goods; for example, radio has succeeded semaphore as a means of communication, and electronic computers now enable economists to estimate models of previously undreamed complexity. A complete survey of progress would therefore need to account in some way for the effect of new goods on the economy. Consumers' tastes must change as their utility functions (or indifference curves) must be redefined to involve more goods, and in consequence the demand for, and the prices of, many existing goods will change. However, in our simplified models we have ignored the possibility of substitution between consumer goods, and so any new variety of corn introduced must completely displace the old. If a bushel of new corn gives more satisfaction to consumers than a bushel of the old although both are produced with the same inputs, consumers will be better off. However, our analysis cannot reflect it unless we equate a bushel of the old with some fraction of a bushel of the new. Then fewer inputs are needed to produce a unit of 'consumer satisfaction', and we have in effect introduced a new method of production in the consumer-satisfaction-producing sector. In this case the introduction of a new type of corn is no different from the discovery of a new method of production, and the consequent effects may be similarly analysed. However, even if we are reluctant to measure the increased satisfaction in so simple a way (if, for example, the extra satisfaction derived from the new corn is less for the rich than for the poor) we can still measure corn output in bushels and remember that the same real wage and level of profits represent a greater level of well-being after the new corn is introduced.

A new type of machine raises rather greater difficulties, because machines are durable and the old machines will stay in use until the stock of new machines is sufficient for all the production planned. The new machines will be used since they produce more cheaply, and so the price of old machines will fall. Capitalists are content to use old machines provided that their price is low enough to give the going profit rate on their investment. The problem of introducing these different *vintages* of durable machines is complex, and we shall return to it briefly at the end of Chapter 13. This type of technical progress involving the introduction of a new type of machine is known as *embodied*, since the economy can only benefit from it if there is investment in new machines in which the improved technology is embodied. Technical progress that comes about from the invention of new ways of combining existing inputs, or from the introduction of new types of consumer goods using similar inputs to the old types, is known as *disembodied* technical progress. It is with disembodied technical progress that we are largely concerned.

11.2 INDUCED AND ENDOGENOUS PROGRESS

In the next chapter we shall allow for the fact that several different improvements may be available, and so we shall discuss the capitalists' choice between them. A considerable literature has grown up discussing whether there is any tendency for there to be a bias in technical progress leading to a persistent tendency for the share of one or other class in national income to rise. We shall see that there are circumstances in which the choice between improved methods of production leaves the distribution unchanged; any tendency for the suppliers of one kind of input to receive a higher price is offset by the choice of a technique that economises on the use of that input. The choice of the improvement is *induced* by changes in the relative prices of inputs in such a way that distributive shares are unchanged.

This induced progress must not be confused with ideas of *endogenous* progress. The technical progress that we have so far discussed (whether embodied or disembodied) is given; the new methods of production may be discovered by research, but we have ignored the resources used in research and development to discover and introduce them. If technical progress is to be made endogenous to the model, we must include research activities and not ignore the resources that they use. We shall also need to include the possibility that very profitable companies may be able to spend more on research than others, so that the pace of technical progress may depend on the profit rate. References to theories of endogenous progress are included in our notes on the literature.

11.3 EFFICIENCY CURVES WITH TECHNICAL PROGRESS: ONE SECTOR

We shall now consider the effect of disembodied progress on the efficiency curve of a one-sector technique. The progress that we shall consider is exogenous; none of the other variables of our model affects the available rate of progress. When several alternative improvements are available capitalists choose between them according to prices, wages and the profit rate, but we shall assume that the range of alternatives that is open to them is not affected by any of these economic variables.

In the one-sector model a tonnes of goods and b man-weeks combine to produce 1 tonne of goods. We shall set the depreciation rate equal to zero for simplicity. When there is technical progress a and b will change over time, and so we shall extend our definitions to say that, in week t, $a(t)$ tonnes of goods and $b(t)$ man-weeks combine to produce 1 tonne of goods. If the stock of goods for use in production at the start of the week t is $S(t)$, output in week t will be $S(t)/a(t)$, and so the labour used will be $b(t)S(t)/a(t)$. Then, if $S(t)$ grows at rate g, consumption output per man-week in week t will be denoted by $c(g, t)$ and given by the formula

$$c(g, t)\frac{S(t)b(t)}{a(t)} + gS(t) = \frac{S(t)}{a(t)}$$

which reduces to a time-dependent version of equation 7 (with $d = 0$):

$$c(g, t) = \frac{1 - ga(t)}{b(t)} \tag{75}$$

Thus the possibilities for consumption and growth are described by the efficiency curve 75, which shifts from week to week. Note that g is defined to be the growth rate of the stock of goods used in production; the growth rate of output will differ from this if the goods requirement $a(t)$ falls over time.

The wage–profit interpretation of the efficiency curve can also be simply determined. With profit rate r the real wage $w(r, t)$ in week t is given by the formula

$$w(r, t)b(t) = 1 - ra(t)$$

which gives the efficiency curve in a form identical to equation 75. Nothing has changed from the analysis of Chapter 2 except that both of the coefficients of production may now depend on time. We know from the analysis of Chapter 4 that the new technique will be chosen in preference to the old only if the efficiency curve for the new technique gives a greater profit rate. If technical progress increases one coefficient whilst reducing the other, there may be an intersection between new and old efficiency curves as in Figure 32. The new technique is superior to the old only for profit rates less than OA and wages above OB. When the profit rate is above OA the new technique is not chosen, and so whether or not a particular invention is a *desired* advance may depend on economic variables as well as on changes in the input requirements. An improvement will of course be unambiguously superior to the old technique if it reduces both the input coefficients.

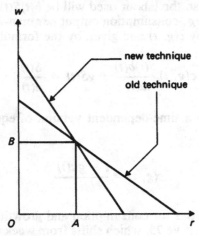

Figure 32

11.4 NEUTRAL PROGRESS IN THE ONE-SECTOR MODEL

So far we have allowed for all combinations of changes in $a(t)$ and $b(t)$. It is often convenient to classify technical progress into *neutral* and *non-neutral* forms, and the three such classifications that have appeared in the literature are easily defined in terms of shifts in efficiency curves.

An improvement in a technique is said to be *Hicks-neutral* progress if the efficiency curve is shifted parallel to itself. Thus in Figure 33, $OC/OD = OE/OF$ and therefore $a(t)$ and $b(t)$ are reduced in the same proportion. The value of k is unchanged by the parallel shift (since in the one-sector model k is the slope of the efficiency curve); and so if r/w is unchanged, the distribution rk/w will be unchanged also.

When there are two or more techniques we say that technical progress is Hicks neutral if each curve is shifted parallel to itself in the same proportion. Thus in Figure 34, progress is Hicks neutral if

$$\frac{OG}{OH} = \frac{OJ}{OK} = \frac{OL}{OM} = \frac{ON}{OP}$$

142

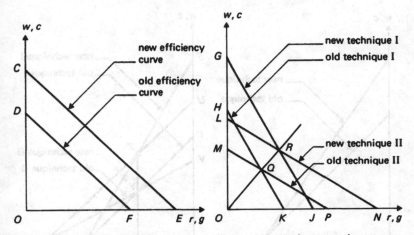

Figure 33 *Hicks-neutral progress*

Figure 34 *Hicks-neutral progress with two techniques*

The input requirements for each technique must be reduced in the same proportion. With such technical progress there is no change in k or in rk/w when r/w is unchanged; the intersections Q of the old curves and R of the new curves are on the same ray through the origin.

A *Harrod-neutral* improvement occurs when $a(t)$ is unchanged and $b(t)$ is reduced, so that the efficiency curve is shifted as in Figure 35. If r is unchanging, profit payments per tonne produced $ra(t)$ will not change from week to week, and so total wage payments $w(r, t)b(t)$ will not change from week to week. Thus, with a fixed profit rate the real wage is increased at the same rate as $b(t)$ is reduced. Also, since $k = a(t)/b(t)$, k will increase at the same rate as $b(t)$ is reduced. Hence, when r is fixed w and k increase at the same rate, and so rk/w is unchanged. When technical progress is Harrod neutral the distribution does not change when the profit rate is constant over time.

When there are several techniques, Harrod-neutral progress occurs when there is an equal proportional reduction in all of the labour inputs $b(t)$ and no change in the goods inputs. So in Figure 36, $OS/OT = OU/OV$ because the two curves are shifted upwards in the same proportion. Point Z is vertically above point Y, and so Harrod-neutral progress does not affect the values of r at which

143

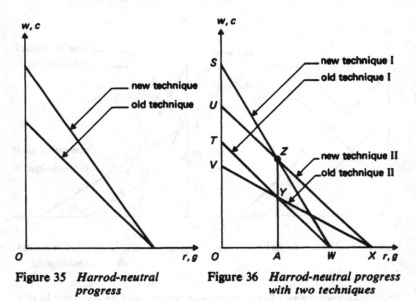

Figure 35 *Harrod-neutral progress*

Figure 36 *Harrod-neutral progress with two techniques*

efficiency curves intersect. When r is between zero and OA, curve TY is chosen before progress and SZ afterwards. These both intersect the r axis at W. Similarly, when r is between OA and OX, the chosen efficiency curve intersects the r axis at X before and after the technical progress has occurred. By the geometry of the one-sector model, the intersection of the efficiency curve with the r axis is equal to the output–capital ratio y/k. Hence if r does not change, the output–capital ratio will be unchanged when progress is Harrod neutral. Thus rk/y is unchanged; and since $w = y - rk$, rk/w is unchanged. So even if there are alternative activities, the distribution will not change when the profit rate is constant, and the technical progress will be of Harrod-neutral form.

Our third definition of neutrality is due to Solow. In this case a single technique is subject to *Solow-neutral* progress if $a(t)$ is reduced with $b(t)$ held constant, so that the efficiency curve shifts as in Figure 37. It is clear from a comparison of Figures 35 and 37 that the Solow-neutral diagram is the same as the Harrod-neutral diagram with the labels on the axes interchanged. Thus, with Solow-neutral progress the distribution is unchanged if the real wage does not change. This result will still hold if there are several

144

techniques each with no change in the labour input and the same rate of reduction in the goods input.

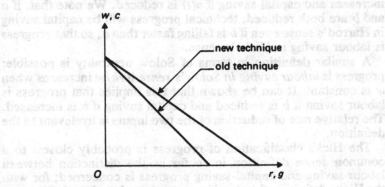

Figure 37 *Solow-neutral progress*

11.5 LABOUR AND CAPITAL-SAVING PROGRESS

Each of these definitions of neutral progress can be used to classify other combinations of changes in $a(t)$ and $b(t)$ into labour-saving and capital-saving forms. Technical progress is *labour saving in Hicks's sense* if, when r/w is constant, less labour is needed, so that the demand for and the price of goods rise relative to the demand for and the price of labour. Hence, rk/w increases, so that the share of wages in national income is reduced. Technical progress is *capital saving in Hicks' sense* if rk/w falls when r/w is constant. These definitions are intuitively reasonable since the ratio of capital to labour, k, must rise when progress is labour saving and fall when it is capital saving. Since $k = a/b$ in the one-sector model, progress is labour saving in Hicks's sense when the labour input falls faster than the goods input for the technique chosen at a fixed value of r/w.

Technical progress is *labour saving in Harrod's sense* if rk/w increases with r constant and is *capital saving in Harrod's sense* if rk/w falls when r is constant. Since rk/w rises and r is constant in this definition of labour-saving progress, k/w rises, and so k/y rises also. Thus, progress is labour saving in Harrod's sense if the capital–output ratio k/y rises when the profit rate is constant. Similarly, if the capital–output ratio falls with r constant, progress will be capital saving in the Harrod sense. Since $k = a/b$ and $y = 1/b$ in the one-sector model, progress is labour saving if $a(t)$ increases and capital saving if $a(t)$ is reduced. We note that, if a and b are both reduced, technical progress will be capital saving in Harrod's sense even if b is falling faster than a, so that progress is labour saving in Hicks's sense.

A similar definition in terms of Solow neutrality is possible: progress is *labour saving in Solow's sense* if rk/w increases when w is constant. It can be shown that this implies that progress is labour saving if b is reduced and capital saving if b is increased. The relative rate of reduction of the two inputs is irrelevant to the definition.

The Hicks classification of progress is probably closest to a common sense definition in so far as the distinction between labour-saving and capital-saving progress is concerned; for with the Hicks definition the classification is based on the relative rates of reduction of the labour and goods inputs, whilst the other two classifications concentrate solely on one of the input requirements. However, we shall see that Harrod neutrality has a more important role on the long-run growth path of the economy, and so the Harrod classification will be of greater use to us in the next chapter.

NOTES ON THE LITERATURE

The effect of technical progress on efficiency curves has been discussed by Schefold (1976), but most of the work in this area has used one-sector models with a production function, as in our appendix to Chapter 4. See, for example, Allen (1967), Jones (1975) and Wan (1971). The definitions used here are analogous to those using production functions and can be translated into the same terminology using the sort of analysis described in the appendix to Chapter 4.

Endogenous progress, in which the rate of improvement depends on the level of investment, was introduced by Kaldor (1957). Black (1962) shows the relation between Kaldor's model and a more conventional model with a production function. Kaldor and Mirrlees (1962) also include endogenous progress, and Arrow (1962) introduces learning by doing in which the accumulation of capital influences the rate of progress. Eltis (1973) provides a discussion of endogenous progress and also of models with embodied progress (see also our section 13.6). Some of the literature in this area is very mathematical. The role of technical progress of various forms in both theory and applied studies has been surveyed by Kennedy and Thirlwall (1973).

The Hicks definition of neutrality originated in Hicks (1932), and Harrod's definition has been used in the analysis of growth in Harrod (1948). Salter (1960) discusses these definitions and biases in progress from both an empirical and a theoretical standpoint. Kennedy (1962), Asimakopulos and Weldon (1963), Asimakopulos (1963) and Sato and Beckmann (1968) also contribute to the classification of technical progress into neutral and non-neutral forms.

CHAPTER 12

Long Run Growth in the One-sector Model

In the previous chapter we defined and classified technical progress. We have not closed the model in any way, and our first task in this chapter is to examine saving behaviour and the labour market in the light of technical progress. We shall then discuss the choice of technique and the possibility of long run growth with Harrod-neutral technical progress.

12.1 SAVING BEHAVIOUR WITH TECHNICAL PROGRESS

In Chapter 5 we used the simplifying assumption that individuals' intertemporal choices can be represented by, at most, three different constant propensities to save. When there is technical progress we must take account of the possibility that all individuals may become richer over time. Production may become more profitable, and so it can be argued that capitalists may wish to save more to take advantage of more profitable opportunities; thus their savings propensity s_c will increase over time. On the other hand, if capitalists foresee the progress, they may save less since they know that they will become richer in the future as production becomes more profitable. If we continue to use a constant value of s_c, we are implicitly assuming that when all capitalists are taken together these two influences cancel each other out. Of course, as progress occurs rk may increase, and a constant s_c is consistent with an increase in the total amount of capitalists' savings per man-week of the labour force. As their incomes rise capitalists may both consume and save more.

We can make a similar assumption about wage earners: that despite increasing real wages they choose to consume a constant proportion of their incomes. We are then assuming that the possibility that their savings propensity increases as they can afford to

148

save more is exactly offset by the tendency for the expectation of greater wages to reduce their need to save to provide for the future. Furthermore, if workers save, they will receive interest on their accumulated assets, and we need to assume similar offsetting motives if we are to have a constant propensity to save out of interest. However, in order to illustrate simply the role of saving in distribution theory when there is technical progress, it is simpler to assume that workers do not save. We therefore avoid all the complications introduced by their saving and the interest on their assets. We shall therefore use the simple relation $g = s_c r$ obtained as equation 48 in section 5.3.

12.2 THE LABOUR MARKET

Apart from the equality of savings and investment we need one more condition to close the model. We are abstracting from uncertainty in our analysis of technical progress, and so the final condition to close the model must be derived from the labour market, as in Chapter 6. We shall examine the implications of assuming that there is continuing full employment. We could examine fixwage theories also, but the assumption of full employment will serve as an illustration of the way in which the theory develops.

We shall suppose in this section that there is only one technique available and that the weekly growth rate of the labour supply is n. Thus, the labour force in week t is $L(0) (1 + n)^t$ where $L(0)$ is the labour force in some initial week 0. If the output of goods in week t is $X(t)$, the full employment condition will be

$$b(t)X(t) = L(0) (1 + n)^t$$

The goods required as inputs are then

$$S(t) = a(t)X(t)$$

so that

$$S(t) = \frac{a(t)L(0) (1 + n)^t}{b(t)} \tag{76}$$

If the growth rate of the stock of goods used in production is g, so that

$$S(t + 1) = (1 + g)S(t)$$

then, from equation 76,

$$\frac{a(t + 1) L(0) (1 + n)^{t+1}}{b(t + 1)} = \frac{a(t) L(0) (1 + n)^t}{b(t)} (1 + g)$$

Hence, the value of g necessary to maintain full employment of the labour force is given by

$$g = (1 + n) \frac{b(t)}{b(t+1)} \times \frac{a(t+1)}{a(t)} - 1 \qquad (77)$$

and if $g = s_c r$, then from the equality of savings and investment we have

$$r = \frac{(1 + n) b(t) a(t + 1)}{s_c b(t + 1) a(t)} - \frac{1}{s_c} \qquad (78)$$

The simplest circumstances in which we can analyse long run growth occur when the same rates of reduction in the input requirements are available each week. So, if $b(t)$ can be reduced by 10 per cent and $a(t)$ by 5 per cent in some week, they can be reduced at these rates in each week. This is clearly a restrictive assumption; a more general model would allow for variable rates of progress from week to week, but we should be unlikely to obtain any easily managed results under a less restrictive condition. Before Chapter 11 we assumed that the same techniques were available in each week; now we have moved a step forward to allow the same rates of improvement from week to week.

The rates of improvement are the rates of change of $b(t)$ and $a(t)$. If these are the same from week to week, the formulae 77 and 78 for g and r will tell us that the growth and profit rates are unchanged from week to week. So we know from section 11.5 that rk/w rises if the improvement is labour saving in Harrod's sense and that the distribution will be unchanging if progress is Harrod neutral. If progress is Harrod neutral, $w(r, t)$ and $y(t)$ will grow at the rate at which $b(t)$ is reduced, and so output in the economy will grow at this rate plus the growth rate of the labour force. We may therefore conclude that, if capitalists save a constant fraction of their incomes, if workers save nothing and if a steadily growing labour force is fully employed, steady growth with an unchanging distribution will be possible if technical progress is Harrod neutral.

12.3 CHOICE OF IMPROVEMENTS

The possibility of steady growth with Harrod-neutral progress is of limited interest unless we can show that capitalists choose a Harrod-neutral improvement in preference to any others available. So in this section we shall consider the choice that capitalists make between improvements. This is analogous to the choice made between alternative techniques in a model without progress; and so, as we shall be using a one-sector model, we shall here be extending section 4.1 to allow for technical progress. Our first extension of that analysis is rather trivial. It is that, if one improvement reduces both a and b faster than a second, the first improvement will always be chosen. This reflects the fact that lower values of both a and b are always advantageous to profit maximisers.

The problem becomes non-trivial when one improvement reduces $a(t)$ faster and $b(t)$ slower than another or vice versa, and this is the case that we shall discuss in the rest of this section. In particular we shall meet a case where an improvement reduces the labour input coefficient faster than does a Harrod-neutral improvement; and so, if the alternative is not unambiguously superior to the neutral improvement, the alternative must increase the goods input coefficient (and hence be labour saving in the Harrod sense). We shall continue to assume that the same possible rates of improvement are available each week.

We shall show that a Harrod-neutral improvement will be chosen in the long run provided that no other improvement that is available reduces both $a(t)$ and $b(t)$ faster than does the neutral improvement. We shall show that the Harrod-neutral improvement increases the real wage faster in the long run than all alternatives and hence will give rise to the outermost efficiency curve. The phrase 'in the long run' is significant since we shall show that there is a maximum number of weeks in which an alternative improvement can be chosen in preference to a neutral improvement, and so the proportion of weeks in which the neutral improvement is chosen increases towards unity as time goes on. So even if there are several alternative improvements available, the fact that none can be used for more than a certain number of weeks implies that the Harrod-neutral improvement must eventually be chosen.

We need some notation to compare a Harrod-neutral improvement with an alternative. We shall use the subscripts N to denote the neutral improvement and A to denote the alternative. Then $b_N(t)$ and $a_N(t)$ are respectively the labour and goods inputs needed to produce 1 tonne of goods after t weeks of the neutral improvement. Similarly, $b_A(t)$ and $a_A(t)$ are the inputs needed after t weeks of the alternative. For a given r the real wage after t weeks of the neutral improvement is $w_N(t)$, and we can similarly define $w_A(t)$. When the alternative improvement is used the price equation for the economy with profit rate r is

$$w_A(t)b_A(t) + ra_A(t) = 1$$

If $w_A(t)b_A(t)$ increases each week, it will eventually exceed unity, making $ra_A(t)$ negative, which is impossible. So eventually (in mathematical terms, in the limit) $w_A(t)$ must increase at a rate no faster than the rate at which $b_A(t)$ is falling:

$$\frac{w_A(t+1)}{w_A(t)} \leqq \frac{b_A(t)}{b_A(t+1)} \tag{79}$$

Now let us suppose that the alternative improvement is always chosen. This will occur only if the alternative shifts the efficiency curve upwards faster than the neutral improvement at the fixed value of r. Thus if the alternative is always chosen,

$$\frac{w_A(t+1)}{w_A(t)} > \frac{w_N(t+1)}{w_N(t)} \tag{80}$$

In Harrod-neutral progress $a_N(t)$ is constant; and so if r is constant, $ra_N(t)$ will be constant, and so profits will be a constant proportion of revenue. Hence, wages $w_N(t)b_N(t)$ must also be a constant proportion of revenue, so that

152

$$\frac{w_N(t + 1)}{w_N(t)} = \frac{b_N(t)}{b_N(t + 1)} \tag{81}$$

A combination of formulae 79, 80 and 81 tells us that, if the alternative is always chosen by the capitalists,

$$\frac{b_A(t)}{b_A(t + 1)} > \frac{b_N(t)}{b_N(t + 1)}$$

Inverting this relationship tells us that $b_A(t + 1)/b_A(t)$ is less than its neutral equivalent. So we have established that, if the alternative improvement is always chosen by the capitalists, the alternative must reduce the labour input faster than the neutral improvement will.

We are analysing a situation in which the alternative improvement does not reduce both input requirements faster than does the neutral improvement. So since the alternative has been shown to reduce the labour input more quickly, it must reduce the goods input more slowly that the neutral improvement. The neutral improvement does not change $a_N(t)$, and so the alternative must increase $a_A(t)$. The alternative improvement must be labour saving in Harrod's sense if it is to increase the real wage faster than the neutral improvement and so be chosen by the capitalists when the profit rate is set by equation 78. With r constant and $a_A(t)$ increasing, the profit payment will continue to increase until it exceeds the revenue. This is plainly impossible. Figure 38 illustrates the situation geometrically. The alternative improvement increases $a_A(t)$, and so the intercept of the efficiency curve with the horizontal axis moves towards the origin, and eventually the profit rate OA is inconsistent with a non-negative wage. CB is the efficiency curve in week t, ED is the curve in week $(t + 1)$ if the alternative improvement is used, and GF is the efficiency curve after two weeks of the alternative. By this time the intercept at F is between the origin and the given profit rate. Meanwhile, the neutral improvement has shifted the curve to HB and then to JB without shifting the intercept B.

We have therefore shown that, if the alternative does not reduce both the input coefficients faster than the neutral improvement, there will be an upper limit to the number of weeks in which the alternative can be used. This upper limit is the number of weeks before the horizontal intercept of the efficiency curve is to the left

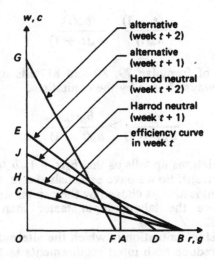

Figure 38

of the profit rate. Even if several alternative improvements were available, a similar result could be shown provided that no combination of the alternatives could reduce $a(t)$ and $b(t)$ faster than the neutral improvement. Thus, the result will hold provided that we cannot use some sequence of the alternatives (such as alternative I in odd weeks and alternative II in even weeks) that reduces the input requirements faster than continued use of the neutral improvement. The result of our analysis will then imply that there is a maximum number of weeks in which each alternative can be used and that, after the sum of these has passed, the Harrod-neutral improvement must be chosen.

These conclusions are very similar to those of the theory of *induced bias* (see notes on the literature). In that theory it is also shown that there is a tendency towards Harrod-neutral progress and a constant distribution. The theory usually uses a continuous *innovation possibility function* to describe an infinity of possible alternative improvements, but even so it is possible to show that the economy will approach a Harrod-neutral growth path. Just as we need to assume that the same rates of improvement are available from week to week, so the theory of induced bias requires that the innovation possibility function is unchanging over time.

154

12.4 CONCLUSIONS

In this chapter we have shown that long run growth with an unchanging distribution is a theoretical possibility and that capitalists receiving a constant profit will chose the Harrod-neutral improvement that is necessary for that growth path. It is possible that the use of alternative improvements may temporarily change the profit rate, but our savings assumption then implies that the growth rate of the goods used in production must also vary, and it is unlikely that such variations in the growth rate will be consistent with continued full employment. Thus, such variations in r are unlikely to continue for many weeks; but even with a constant r our conclusions rest on certain basic assumptions.

First, we have only one sector. We shall discuss an extension of the results of this chapter to the two-sector model in Chapter 13, where we shall discover that the economy may not necessarily converge to a Harrod-neutral growth path. We have assumed also that technical progress is disembodied, so that the improvements are available to those who use goods produced a long time ago as well as to those using recently produced goods. We discussed this to some extent in section 11.1, and we shall do so again in the next chapter. Disembodied progress is usually assumed in induced bias theory, and it has the effect that the economy can respond quickly to cost-saving inventions; for if progress is embodied, so that only newly produced inputs benefit from improvements, the old machines cannot be changed in any way to respond to changes in input prices. Little work has been done on induced bias with embodied progress, but it is plausible to argue that an increase in the wage will tend to increase the workers' share because it is not possible to economise on the labour used with old goods. Thus, the tendency to economise on expensive inputs is reduced, and so the movement towards a constant distribution may be slowed.

We have already discussed the assumption that the same rates of improvement are available for a large number of weeks. This assumption allows us to see the influence of technical progress on the distribution, but it does not tell us how changes in the rate of progress affect the distribution. In particular our assumption avoids the necessity to incorporate entrepreneurs' expectations of progress in the model since it is assumed that they know the available constant rates of improvement. A theory reflecting more of the complexities of the economy would need to include different rates of improvement in different weeks. It would also need to reintroduce the entrepreneurial income of Chapter 10 as the reward to those who are clever enough, or lucky enough, to foresee future changes in technology and to predict their effects on prices and profitability.

We are further assuming in our analysis that all capitalists are able to introduce an improvement at the same time. No monopoly benfits accrue in the model to those who are first to introduce a new technology, and there is no scope for the exercise of patent rights by inventors. In a more general model attention must be paid to the rate at which new knowledge is diffused through the economy.

The theory of induced bias was originally put forward to explain the constancy of the distribution. Our version of the theory involves efficiency curves, but criticisms made of the approach using an innovation possibility function apply also to our theory. All the points made in this section weaken the value of the theory for explaining the distribution, and a more general model must account for some or all of them; but however we may wish to modify the assumptions, any theory involving profit-seeking entrepreneurs must account for their desire to economise on costs and their consequent tendency to seek to improve the technique of production in the most profitable way. The sort of theory that we have put forward is a first approximation to the role of such behaviour in determining the distribution, just as, for example, the use of savings propensities is an approximation that is useful for analysing the role of time preference in distribution theory.

NOTES ON THE LITERATURE

Many of the references to the previous chapter deal also with issues raised in this chapter. The theory of induced bias was introduced to the modern literature by Kennedy (1964), who attributes the first ideas to Hicks (1932). Samuelson (1965) introduces a production function and also discusses alternative assumptions on the long run behaviour of capitalists. Kennedy (1966) and Samuelson (1966c) discuss the relation between their two approaches, and Chang (1972) discusses interpretations of the innovation possibility function.

CHAPTER 13

Technical Progress in Other Models

We have analysed in detail technical progress in the one-sector model; but as we have seen in earlier chapters, this has many limitations. In particular there is no scope for price changes or variations in the balance between sectors. The problem with the analysis of technical progress in two-sector and more complicated models is that the algebraic manipulation is much less easy. In this chapter we shall introduce some of the theory of the previous chapters to the two-sector and Austrian models, but we shall not analyse them in detail. However, there are some important issues that we must develop to some extent.

In the first section we shall discuss the possibility of price changes in some detail and, in particular, concentrate on expectations of these changes. We shall then see what effect these expectations have on our measures of distribution derived from the national accounts. The Austrian model can be used to illustrate some other problems, and we shall do this in the third section. In the fourth section we shall extend our definitions of neutral progress, and in the fifth section we shall see how a Harrod-neutral growth path may arise. We shall also see that the balance between the outputs of the two sectors may not adjust to make neutral progress and steady growth possible. Finally, we shall make some remarks on the introduction of embodied progress to the two-sector model.

13.1 THE TWO-SECTOR MODEL

THE QUANTITY CURVE

In the two-sector model disembodied progress causes the coefficients α, β, a and b to change over time. If the progress occurs in only one of the sectors, two of the coefficients will remain the same, but this possibility can easily be incorporated into the more general analysis.

The quantity equations analogous to equations 17 and 18 in the model without progress are

$$a(t)x(t) + \alpha(t)\xi(t) = S(t)$$

$$b(t)x(t) + \beta(t)\xi(t) = L(t)$$

Defining $g(t)$ to be the growth rate of the tractor stock from week t to week $(t + 1)$ gives

$$x(t) = gS(t)$$

and so the quantity efficiency curve is

$$c[g(t), t] = \frac{\xi(t)}{L(t)} = \frac{1 - g(t)a(t)}{\beta(t) + g(t)[\alpha(t)b(t) - \beta(t)a(t)]}$$

which is in exactly the same form as the curve without progress except that the input coefficients and g now depend on time. We notice that the growth rate of national output per man-week need no longer equal $g(t)$, since the tractor stock grows at $g(t)$ and fewer tractors may now be needed per man-week of labour in both sectors.

THE PRICE CURVE

When we examine the price equations for each sector we must take account of changes in the price ratio p/π as well as of changes in the real wage. Furthermore, because prices and wages change, individuals will have expectations of these changes. These expectations will help to determine individual behaviour, and so we need some theory of how expectations are formed. We shall first examine how expectations of price changes enter into the calculations of profit maximisers and then discuss the formation of expectations and the consequences of incorrectly predicting price changes.

We shall assume that wage earners contract with capitalists to receive a money wage $w_m(t)$ at the end of week t. The money prices of tractors and corn are $p(t)$ and $\pi(t)$ respectively at the start of the week and are expected to become $p^e(t)$ and $\pi^e(t)$ respectively at the end of the week. The owner of a tractor therefore expects to make a capital gain $[p^e(t) - p(t)]$ on his tractor (for simplicity we are assuming that there is no depreciation). A capitalist producing one tractor has a wage bill of $w_m(t)b(t)$ and an expected revenue of $p^e(t)$. He also expects a gain of $[p^e(t) - p(t)]a(t)$ on the tractors that he uses, and these must enter his account of the profitability of tractor production. His expected profit including his capital gains is

$$p^e(t) + [p^e(t) - p(t)]a(t) - w_m(t)b(t)$$

and so his expected profit rate on the initial investment of $p(t)a(t)$ is

$$r^e(t) = \frac{p^e(t) + [p^e(t) - p(t)]a(t) - w_m(t)b(t)}{p(t)a(t)}$$

Likewise, in the corn sector the expected profit rate is

$$\rho^e(t) = \frac{\pi^e(t) + [p^e(t) - p(t)]\alpha(t) - w_m(t)\beta(t)}{p(t)\alpha(t)}$$

In the absence of monopolistic barriers to entry in one of the sectors the economy can only be in equilibrium if $r^e(t) = \rho^e(t)$. Otherwise, capitalists will move resources into the sector that they expect to be more profitable. So in equilibrium we have the two price equations

$$p^e(t) = w_m(t)b(t) + r^e(t)p(t)a(t) - [p^e(t) - p(t)]a(t) \qquad (82)$$

$$\pi^e(t) = w_m(t)\beta(t) + r^e(t)p(t)\alpha(t) - [p^e(t) - p(t)]\alpha(t) \qquad (83)$$

These equations cannot be manipulated easily into a price efficiency curve unless we make a substitution. We define $r(t)$ by the equation

$$r(t) = \frac{r^e(t)p(t) - [p^e(t) - p(t)]}{p^e(t)} \qquad (84)$$

159

This somewhat artificial variable reflects both the expected profit rate and the price expectations and it can be interpreted as the rate of return net of capital gains that capitalists expect to receive on their assets, valued at the price expected at the end of the week. By substituting $r(t)$ into equations 82 and 83 and dividing through by $\pi^e(t)$ we obtain an expression for the expected real wage $w^e(t)$ in terms of $r(t)$:

$$w^e[r(t), t] = \frac{1 - r(t)a(t)}{\beta(t) + r(t)[\alpha(t)b(t) - \beta(t)a(t)]}$$

We see that the expected real wage is the same function of $r(t)$ as consumption output per man-week is of the growth rate of the tractor stock. We should note, however, that the variable $r(t)$ is not the profit rate on which the capitalists base their calculations; $r(t)$ depends on that profit rate and also on the expected change in the price of tractors.

THE FORMATION OF EXPECTATIONS

The price and quantity efficiency curves are in identical form, but before we examine the national accounts and the distribution we should discuss the forces that determine individuals' price expectations.

Expectations can be formed in a variety of ways. For example, individuals may be naive and believe that there will be no change in prices, so that $p^e(t) = p(t)$ and $\pi^e(t) = \pi(t)$. In this case there is no expectation of capital gain, and $r(t) = r^e(t)$. Alternatively, individuals may expect that the change in prices during week t will be the same as that experienced in week $(t - 1)$, so that

$$p^e(t) - p(t) = p(t) - p(t - 1)$$

and similarly for the price of corn. More generally, the expected price change may be a weighted average of many past price changes, so that $p^e(t)$ and $\pi^e(t)$ are functions of many past prices. Finally, in models of predictable steady-state growth it may be possible to assume that price changes can be accurately forecast. Then the expected prices may be taken to be equal to their actual values at the start of week $(t + 1)$ (which is the same instant at the end of week t), so that $p^e(t) = p(t + 1)$ and $\pi^e(t) = \pi(t + 1)$.

Except in this last case of perfect foresight, expectations may not be borne out. In this case the owner of tractors will make an unexpected gain or loss, and the workers' real wage will differ from that expected. Technical progress can therefore lead to uncertainty, and a full analysis of the effects of progress should allow for entrepreneurial income as in Chapter 10; for then the entrepreneurs can take the risks (for this is their function), and the workers and capitalists can make contracts in real terms, so that their incomes are unaffected by unexpected variations in prices. In this case the money wage contract will be the real wage $w(t)$ multiplied by the price of corn actually occurring at the end of week t, which is $\pi(t + 1)$. Similarly, capitalists could rent out their machines for a fixed real return including the capital gains that actually occur during the week.

13.2 THE FUNCTIONAL DISTRIBUTION WITH PROGRESS

The possibility of unfulfilled expectations complicates the analysis of distribution. We shall restrict ourselves to examining whether the efficiency curve analysis of earlier chapters can be adapted to say anything useful about the distribution even though it now relates the expected wage to the variable $r(t)$ and not the actual wage to the profit rate.

If we retain the assumption used in Chapters 11 and 12 that workers do not save, capitalists expect to consume $(c - w^e)$ bushels of corn per man-week employed at the end of week t (note that we drop the argument (t) from our variables as we are concerned only with week t in this section). In money terms they expect to spend $(c - w^e)\pi^e$ on corn. The money value of the tractor stock at the start of the week is pS, and by the end of the week the stock will have grown at rate g, and the price is expected to change to p^e. Thus the value of the tractor stock is expected to be $p^eS(1 + g)$, and investment (defined as the change in the value of the tractor stock) is $[p^e(1 + g) - p]S$. Capitalists expect a profit rate or r^e and total profits r^epS, which is to be spent on consumption and investment. So, measured per man-week, the capitalists' expected income and expenditure are

$$\frac{r^e pS}{L} = \frac{(1 + g)p^eS}{L} - \frac{pS}{L} + (c - w^e)\pi^e \qquad (85)$$

161

Substituting using equation 84 gives

$$(r - g) \frac{p^e S}{\pi^e L} = c - w^e$$

and hence the ratio $(c - w^e)/(r - g)$ is equal to the current capital stock per man-week valued in terms of corn at the prices that are expected to rule at the end of the week. We shall denote this valuation of the stock by k^e to emphasise that it is an *ex ante* expectation of the value at the end of the week. Figure 39 illustrates the efficiency curve for week t, and k^e is given by the slope of BD. The ratio of AB to OA, which normally measures the functional distribution in these diagrams, is not quite so straightforward to interpret in this case; for $rk^e = rp^e S / \pi^e L$ and from equation 84 this is equal to $[r^e p - (p^e - p)]S/\pi^e L$, which is the profits that capitalists expect to receive apart from their capital gains, measured as the number of bushels of corn that capitalists expect to be able to buy. Thus rk^e/w^e is the ratio of *expected profits minus capital gains to the expected real wage*.

It is useful to have a measure of profits minus capital gains because an amount of saving equal to the gains is always needed to equal the amount of investment that the gains represent. If capital-

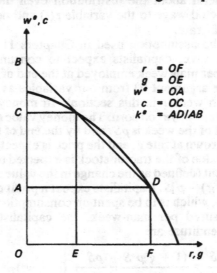

$$\begin{aligned} r &= OF \\ g &= OE \\ w^e &= OA \\ c &= OC \\ k^e &= AD/AB \end{aligned}$$

Figure 39

162

ists attempt to spend any of their capital gains, the amount of saving net of total capital gains will be reduced. This is a familiar real-world problem, as an individual may sell his shares in a company to realise and spend his capital gains. If he does so, someone else must save to buy these shares, and then less of his savings will be available to finance new investment by buying new issues of shares. Thus, the measure of profits minus capital gains tells us how much the capitalist class is able to spend on consumption goods and new equipment given that some capitalists must always save to cover capital gains.

13.3 PROGRESS IN AUSTRIAN MODELS

Other problems that arise when we try to incorporate technical progress into more complicated models can be seen when we examine the Austrian model of section 2.3. In week t a process started two weeks previously produces one bushel of corn; a process started one week previously requires an input of $b_2(t)$ man-weeks; and a process started in week t requires $b_1(t)$ man-weeks. If the number of processes started in week t is $h(t)$, the requirement of labour in week t is $[b_1(t)h(t) + b_2(t)h(t-1)]$ man-weeks. Consumption output is $h(t-2)$, and so consumption output per man-week $c(t)$ is given by

$$h(t-2) = c(t)[b_1(t)h(t) + b_2(t)h(t-1)] \qquad (86)$$

The only way in which $c(t)$ can be related to a single growth rate g is

$$\text{if } h(t) = (1+g)h(t-1)$$

and

$$h(t-1) = (1+g)h(t-2)$$

so that the growth rate of the number of processes started is the same for two successive weeks. If, more generally, these growth rates differ, so that

$$h(t) = (1+g_1)h(t-1)$$

163

and

$$h(t - 1) = (1 + g_2)h(t - 2)$$

equation 86 gives a formula for $c(t)$ in terms of two growth rates rather than one:

$$c(g_1, g_2, t) = \frac{1}{b_2(t)(1 + g_2) + b_1(t)(1 + g_1)(1 + g_2)} \quad (87)$$

A similar problem arises when we consider wages and profits. A process begun in week t incorporates an investment $w_m(t)b_1(t)$ in labour paid at the end of the week, so that a capitalist beginning a process in week t would expect to be able to sell the right to operate a part-time process for a price $p_1^e(t)$ where

$$p_1^e(t) = w_m(t)b_1(t) \quad (88)$$

Likewise, a capitalist could buy a one-week-old process for $p_1(t)$ at the start of week t, expect to earn a profit at rate $r^e(t)$ on that investment, add to it a payment of $w_m(t)b_2(t)$ to labour, and sell a two-week-old process at the end of week t for an expected price $p_2^e(t)$. Thus

$$p_2^e 1(t) = [1 + r^e(t)]p_1(t) + w_m(t)b_2(t) \quad (89)$$

Finally, a capitalist could buy a two-week-old process at the start of week t for $p_2(t)$ and expect to receive a profit at rate $r^e(t)$. Such a two-week-old process yields an expected revenue of $\pi^e(t)$ from the sale of a bushel of corn at the end of the week. Hence

$$\pi^e(t) = p_2(t)[1 + r^e(t)] \quad (90)$$

In the two-sector model we eliminated the variable r^e from the price equations by defining r in equation 84. In this model we need to define two variables r_1 and r_2 in a similar way:

$$r_1(t) = \frac{[1 + r^e(t)]p_1(t)}{p_1^e(t)}$$

164

$$r_2(t) = \frac{[1 + r^e(t)]p_2(t)}{p_2^e(t)}$$

and then the price equations 88, 89 and 90 can be simplified to give

$$w^e(r_1, r_2, t) = \frac{w_m(t)}{\pi^e(t)} = \frac{1}{b_2(t)(1 + r_2) + b_1(t)(1 + r_1)(1 + r_2)} \qquad (91)$$

which is of similar form to equation 87. The expected real wage is a function of both r_1 and r_2, and these may be different according to the ways in which the price expectations $p_1^e(t)$ and $p_2^e(t)$ arise. The efficiency curves are no longer in two dimensions, and the simple representation of the national accounts given in Chapter 3 is no longer possible. A similar problem arises in models with more than one capital good. The stock of each capital good may grow at a different rate, and the formation of price expectations may mean that the variables r_i, defined for each type of capital good in the same way as r is defined in the two-sector model, may differ also.

13.4 NEUTRAL PROGRESS

In this section we shall extend the definitions of neutral progress to models in which the efficiency curve is not a straight line although it can still be represented in two dimensions. Neutral progress in the one-sector model implies that the distribution does not change when r/w (Hicks), r (Harrod) or w (Solow) is unchanged from one week to the next. In the two-sector model the measure of distribution derived from the efficiency curve diagram is rk^e/w^e; and as we saw in section 13.3, this is the ratio of expected profits minus capital gains to the expected real wage. For convenience we shall refer to this as the *expected distribution*.

The main addition that we must make to our definitions stems from the fact that k^e depends on g as well as r when the efficiency curve is non-linear. Progress is Hicks neutral if the expected distribution does not change when w^e/r and c/g are unchanged from week to week. This will occur when the curve shifts in the manner shown in Figure 40 where

$$OG/OH = OJ/OK = OL/OM = ON/OP$$

Then if r changes from OQ to OR, w^e will change from OW to OX. If g changes from OS to OT, c will change from OU to OV. The slope of PM is the same as the slope of NL since the triangles OPM and ONL are similar. Thus k^e is unchanged, and so is rk^e/w^e.

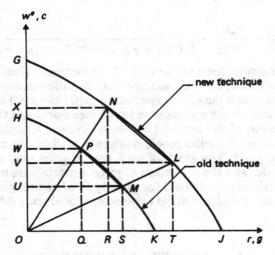

Figure 40   *Hicks-neutral progress – two-sector model*

Progress is Harrod neutral if the expected distribution is unchanged when r and g are unchanged. In Figure 41 the curve shifts upwards by a constant proportion, so that

$$OH/OG = AC/AB = DF/DE$$

Then if r remains at OA and g at OD, c will rise by BC and w^e by EF, so that k^e will change from the slope of BE to the slope of CF and $(w^e + rk^e)$ will change by GH. Thus w^e and rk^e change by the same proportion.

Progress is Solow neutral if rk^e/w^e is unchanged when w^e and c^e are unchanged. This is illustrated in Figure 42 where

$$QS/QR = MP/MN = OL/OK$$

so that the curve has shifted horizontally by a constant proportion.

166

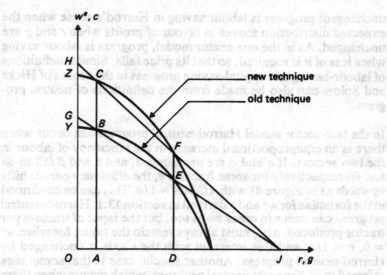

Figure 41 *Harrod-neutral progress – two-sector model*

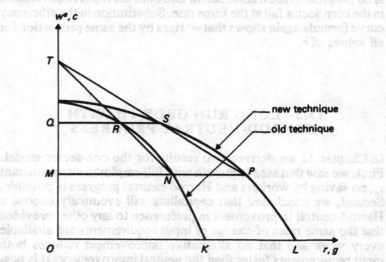

Figure 42 *Solow-neutral progress – two-sector model*

From these definitions we can derive definitions of labour-saving and capital-saving technical progress. For example, progress is capital saving in Harrod's sense if rk^e/w^e falls when r and g are

167

unchanged; progress is labour saving in Harrod's sense when the expected distribution moves in favour of profits when r and g are unchanged. As in the one-sector model, progress is labour saving when less of it is required, so that its price falls. Similar definitions of labour-saving and capital-saving progress in the senses of Hicks and Solow can also be made from the definitions of neutral progress.

In the two-sector model Harrod-neutral progress can occur when there is an equiproportional increase in the efficiency of labour in the two sectors. If a and α are unchamged, and b and β fall to θb and $\theta\beta$ respectively for some fraction θ, the efficiency curve shifts upwards as in Figure 41 with $AC/AB = 1/\theta$. This can be confirmed in the formulae for w^e and c derived in section 13.1. Harrod-neutral progress can occur in other ways too, but the input of tractors per tractor produced, $a(t)$, must always remain the same; for when $w^e = 0$, $r = 1/a$, and this intercept with the r axis is unchanged by Harrod-neutral progress. Another special case is that sometimes referred to as *Kennedy-neutral progress*, which occurs when there is no progress in the tractor sector and both the input requirements in the corn sector fall at the same rate. Substitution in the efficiency curve formula again shows that w^e rises by the same proportion for all values of r.

13.5 LONG RUN GROWTH WITH HARROD-NEUTRAL PROGRESS

In Chapter 12 we derived two results for the one-sector model. First, we saw that steady growth with full employment, a constant s_c, no saving by workers and Harrod-neutral progress is possible. Second, we concluded that capitalists will eventually choose a Harrod-neutral improvement in preference to any other provided that the same rates of change of input requirements are available every week and that no alternative improvement reduces both input requirements faster than the neutral improvement. It is possible in some circumstances to extend these results to two-sector models, but we have two extra considerations to examine. We must take account of price expectations and of changes in the fraction of the labour force employed in each sector.

PRICE EXPECTATIONS

If the economy is growing steadily, its behaviour can be easily predicted. The economy is moving in a regular way, the efficiency of labour is improving at a constant rate, and it is not unreasonable to assume that the individuals can predict price changes correctly, so that $p^e(t) = p(t + 1)$ and $\pi^e(t) = \pi(t + 1)$. There is then no unforeseen entrepreneurial income (positive or negative), and saving and investment decisions based on expected prices and profit rates are actually borne out. It is therefore possible to plan for full employment without fear of a deficiency of demand caused by unforeseen price movements.

If individuals do predict prices correctly, it can be shown that long-run steady growth is possible in the two-sector model with Harrod-neutral progress, $r = g/s_c$ and full employment. The values of r and g do not change, and so the expected distribution (which is the actual distribution net of capital gains with perfect foresight) does not change either. We can see this most easily in the case where b and β fall to θb and $\theta \beta$ respectively with a and α unchanged. In this case the labour force is growing steadily in efficiency; and if it is also growing steadily in size, the fraction of the labour force employed in each sector can remain the same, and the two outputs can grow at the same rate. A similar result can be shown if the Harrod-neutral progress arises in other ways.

OUTPUTS OF THE TWO SECTORS

It is possible to show that the capitalists will choose the Harrod-neutral improvement in the same circumstances as in the one-sector model. They may choose the alternative for a few weeks, but eventually the alternative improvement will shift the efficiency curve in such a way that it is no longer compatible with a fixed value of r, exactly as in the one-sector model in Figure 38. The main problem is that, when the period of uninterrupted neutral progress begins, the actual ratio of tractors to labour available may not equal that needed for steady growth. If the actual ratio is greater than the steady growth ratio, full employment will require that more resources be employed in the more tractor-intensive sector than steady growth will require. If $\alpha(t)/\beta(t) > a(t)/b(t)$, the corn sector will be the more tractor intensive, and the existence of more tractors than are needed will imply that corn output is increased and tractor output reduced from their steady growth levels. There is a tendency in the economy to reduce the ratio of tractors to labour by reducing the output of tractors. Thus, the initial excess of tractors will tend to disappear. However, if the tractor sector is the more tractor intensive, the extra tractors can only be used if the output of tractors is increased above the level needed for steady growth. The surplus of tractors will tend to increase, and the economy will not move towards its steady growth path. Thus, the economy moves towards the steady growth path only if $\alpha/\beta > a/b$.

This analysis is similar to the stability arguments used by Hicks (1965) where he discusses the *traverse* from one growth path to another in a model without technical progress. When there is a tendency away from the steady growth path, full employment cannot continue for ever, and some other forces must be involved in determining the path that the economy follows. This causal indeterminacy in the model leads to many complications that we cannot pursue here.

13.6 EMBODIED TECHNICAL PROGRESS

The problem of analysing embodied technical progress – wherein improvements in the technology can only be achieved by investing in new machines – is very much more complicated than its disembodied counterpart. This generally leads to the use of much more complex algebra and calculus than we have met so far, but by making certain simplifying assumptions we can introduce the issues involved and point to certain of the problems.

Let us suppose that in a two-sector model a new type of tractor is invented. Then b_n labour using a_n new tractors can produce one new tractor, and β_n labour using α_n tractors can produce one bushel of corn. Old tractors are still in existence and can be used to make new tractors (inputs β_o and α_o) and corn (inputs b_o and a_o). Old tractors can also be used to make old tractors, but we shall assume that the demand for these never exceeds the stock available when the new tractors are invented. For simplicity we shall assume that all the old coefficients exceed their new counterparts (so that $a_o > a_n$, and so on), although it is possible to develop a theory in which some inputs are reduced at the expense of increasing others. As with disembodied progress this possibility may lead to ambiguity in deciding whether the new methods actually represent an improvement on the old (see Figure 32 in section 11.3).

The main problem that arises when there are different vintages of tractors is the expectation that there will be further inventions that may render currently 'new' tractors obsolete. Even if tractors do not depreciate physically, they will be scrapped if some future inventor devises an even more efficient brand of tractor. Thus, capitalists will expect to receive an income only for a few weeks and will want to receive an income to cover this obsolescence. For example, suppose that the profit rate is r, that the price of new tractors is p_n and that the owner of one new tractor expects to have a weekly income of q_n from it for T weeks, after which it is obsolete. The stream of incomes q_n must cover profits rp_n per week plus the repayment of the original cost p_n. So if his flow of income is discounted to the week in which he buys the new tractor, we have

$$\sum_{t=1}^{T} \frac{q_n}{(1+r)^t} = p_n$$

so that

$$q_n = rp_n \bigg/ \left(1 - \frac{1}{(1+r)^T}\right) \tag{92}$$

The price equations for the two activities using new tractors are

$$q_n a_n + w_m b_n = p_n \tag{93}$$

$$q_n \alpha_n + w_m \beta_n = \pi \tag{94}$$

since anyone seeking to use a new tractor must pay its owner q_n. Equations 92, 93 and 94 can be solved to determine the real wage, p_n/π and q_n/π in terms of the profit rate.

Old tractors will be used as long as they are productive enough to earn revenue to cover wage costs. For example, if old tractors are to be used in the corn sector, revenue net of wage payments will be $(\pi - w_m \beta_o)$. Revenue per tractor used is the expression

$$\frac{\pi - w_m \beta_o}{\alpha_o} \tag{95}$$

whilst in the tractor sector the revenue per old tractor used to produce a new tractor is

171

$$\frac{p_n - w_m b_o}{a_o} \tag{96}$$

Old tractors will be used to produce corn if expression 95 is positive and exceeds expression 96, and they will be used to produce new tractors if expression 96 is positive and exceeds expression 95. If neither expression 95 nor expression 96 is positive, old tractors will not be used.

In more general circumstances there may be three or more vintages of tractors in existence, and older vintages will be used as long as they can earn some surplus over the cost of labour and other inputs such as raw materials, for then their owners have an incentive to use the older tractors rather than to scrap them. There is no difficulty other than extra notation in incorporating many vintages into the model, and we can then use expressions similar to expressions 95 and 96 to indicate which vintage will be used and hence the age of the oldest vintage still in use.

Greater difficulties arise when we recognise that the expectations involved in equation 92 are of a very simple form. In more general circumstances entrepreneurs would expect future inventions and hence lower profits from their current equipment. They would then expect a declining income in the future rather than a constant stream of q_n per week. These expectations are likely to be based on their past experience, and so the expected price of tractors in the future will depend on past prices, giving rise to much more complicated price equations than those used here. The principles involved remain largely the same, as the owners of old tractors receive lower incomes than those with new tractors and some tractors become obsolete, but the formal analysis is much more complicated. We shall not pursue it here.

NOTES ON THE LITERATURE

Technical progress in two-sector models has been discussed by Diamond (1965), Takayama (1965) and Findlay (1967), whilst induced bias in two-sector models has been introduced by von Weizsacker (1966) and McCain (1972). The stability of such a model has been discussed by Craven (1973). Technical progress in multisectoral models has been discussed by Burmeister and Dobell (1969), Kennedy (1973), Orosel (1977) and Craven (1978). Wan (1971) and Eltis (1973) discuss embodied progress and models with

172

several vintages of capital goods. The bulk of the work in this area has used a one-sector model.

CHAPTER 14

Conclusions

In the first six chapters we built up a macroeconomic model to expose the main forces determining the functional distribution of income. This model consists of three main parts: a summary of the technology (the efficiency curve), intertemporal behaviour (saving and investment) and the labour market. The introduction of skilled labour, land, uncertainty and technical progress has modified the analysis but has not changed the role of technology and intertemporal behaviour in the determination of the distribution. The introduction of uncertainty has enabled us to develop a Keynesian model in which the money market replaces the labour market as the third part of the model, but we still have a macroeconomic theory.

We modified the basic model by including only one development at a time, but it is possible to build up a model containing all the features of Chapters 9–13 without altering the structure of the model. The algebra involved in such a model would be very complicated, and it is unlikely that any greater insight would be gained into the way in which the economy works. We could also introduce more goods to the model, produced jointly or each in a different sector, and we could make the structure of the time lags between inputs and outputs very complex. Several of our references deal with these more complicated models, but the essential points are that we can still derive an efficiency curve as a summary of the technology and that this efficiency curve can still be used in a macroeconomic theory of distribution. As we have indicated on numerous occasions throughout the book, the most important development is the move from a one-sector model with a linear efficiency curve to a two-sector or an Austrian model.

If we wish to develop our understanding of the forces determining the distribution beyond the analysis of this book, there are two roads that we can follow. One road takes us back towards the general equilibrium analysis discussed in Chapter 1. We could introduce some 'feedbacks' into the apparent causal structures described in sections 1.3 (Figures 2 and 3) and 10.3 (Figure 31). One of the main features of the macroeconomic approach is the separation of the analysis of the technology from that of saving behaviour. A general equilibrium model allows 'everything to depend on everything else', so that it is impossible to complete the analysis of one part of the economy before moving on to another.

The second way in which we can develop the model involves the use of partial-equilibrium microeconomic analysis to add detail to the general structure of the macro model. For example, we have seen how wage differentials can be fitted into the macroeconomic model, but a more detailed analysis of the individual choices between occupations and the demands for various kinds of skills is best made by concentrating on only a small part of the economy. It is possible to examine these details in isolation now that we know from the macro model how differentials fit into the determination of the distribution in the economy as a whole.

The return towards general equilibrium and the use of partial equilibrium additions to the macroeconomic framework can give us extra insights, but there are some problems with the macro analysis that must be mentioned. We have considered the distribution of income when the economy is in macroeconomic and microeconomic equilibrium, and we have dealt only with an economy whose technology has constant returns to scale.

Macroeconomic equilibrium is introduced through the use of the condition that savings equal investment (and this could be modified in the presence of foreign trade or government activity). Microeconomic equilibrium is introduced through the assumption that the profit rate is the same in both sectors of a two-sector model and hence that capitalists are not induced to move their resources from one sector to another. However, when there is uncertainty or technical progress actual profit rates may not be the same, and plans to save may not be in agreement with plans to invest. Some individuals will therefore find that the actual outcome differs from their plans. There may be forces in the economy that lead it towards equilibrium (prices may change to help equalise profit rates, and a multiplier may change national income and saving), but the economy will not adjust instantaneously, and the distribution will change during the period of adjustment. The interpersonal distribution may be considerably affected as, for example, some activities may turn out to be much more profitable than others. The clever, or the lucky, may be able to gain by buying and selling assets in anticipation of variations in profit rates as the economy moves towards equilibrium.

The second omission from our model is the analysis of increasing returns to scale. These can arise from both physical and organisational sources. A 3-metre-cube water tank requires 54 square metres of metal to enclose it and holds 27 cubic metres; a 6 metre cube has eight times the volume but requires only a fourfold increase in the surrounding metal. In this case we can no longer assume that the input coefficients are independent of the scale of operations, and so the position of the efficiency curve and the size of national income per man-week depend on the scale of operations. Organisational increasing returns arise from extensions of the division of labour through the possibilities of greater specialisation when there is mass production. The available methods of production depend on the sizes of the firms and on the extent of the market for a particular good.

In many ways increasing returns give rise to the same problems as technical progress. It is difficult to separate the introduction of new inventions from the introduction of new methods made possible by growth. However, when we compare large and small countries or examine the consequences of changes in the growth rate (which may enable capitalists to take advantage of increasing returns in one of the sectors), the technology is not changing, but returns to scale are important. We note that decreasing returns are not a problem, since, if a single firm experiences decreasing returns, there can be constant returns in the industry as a whole by having more firms all operating at the optimal size (where average costs are minimised).

We can go no further here; but it must be said that, as soon as we move away from equilibrium analysis with constant returns, many difficulties arise. Most of these difficulties have yet to be solved in distribution theory.

BIBLIOGRAPHY

Allen, R. G. D. (1967) *Macroeconomic Theory* (London: Macmillan).
American Economic Association (1954) *Readings in the Theory of Income Distribution* (London: Allen & Unwin).
American Economic Association and Royal Economic Society (1965) *Surveys of Economic Theory*, Vol. 2 (London: Macmillan).
Arrow, K. J. (1951) *Social Choice and Individual Values* (New York: Wiley).
Arrow, K. J. (1962) 'The economic implications of learning by doing', *Review of Economic Studies*, Vol. 29, pp. 155–73. Also in Newman (1968), Stiglitz and Uzawa (1969) and Hahn (1971).
Arrow, K. J., Chenery, H. B., Minhas, B. S. and Solow, R. M. (1961) 'Capital–labour substitution and economic efficiency', *Review of Economics and Statistics*, Vol. 43, pp. 225–48. Also in Harcourt and Laing (1971).
Arrow, K. J. and Hahn, F. H. (1971) *General Competitive Analysis* (Edinburgh: Oliver & Boyd).
Asimakopulos, A. (1963) 'The definition of neutral improvements', *Economic Journal*, Vol. 73, pp. 675–80.
Asimakopulos, A. and Weldon, J. C. (1963) 'The classification of technical progress in models of economic growth', *Economica*, Vol. 30, pp. 372–86.
Atkinson, A. B. (1972) *Unequal Shares: Wealth in Britain* (London: Allen Lane).
Atkinson, A. B. (1975) *The Economics of Inequality* (Oxford: Clarendon Press).
Atkinson, A. B. (ed.) (1976) *The Personal Distribution of Incomes* (London: Allen & Unwin).
Atsumi, H. (1960) 'Mr Kaldor's theory of income distribution', *Review of Economic Studies*, Vol. 27, pp. 109–18.
Bacharach, M. (1976) *Economics and the Theory of Games* (London: Macmillan).
Baranzini, M. (1975) 'The Pasinetti and anti-Pasinetti theorems: a reconciliation', *Oxford Economic Papers*, Vol. 27, pp. 470–2.
Baumol, W. J. (1961) *Economic Theory and Operations Analysis* (London: Prentice Hall).
Becker, G. S. (1975) *Human Capital* (New York: Columbia University Press).
Bhaduri, A. (1969) 'On the significance of recent controversies in capital theory: a Marxian view', *Economic Journal*, Vol. 79, pp. 532–9. Also in Harcourt and Laing (1971).
Black, J. (1962) 'The technical progress function and the production function', *Economica*, Vol. 29, pp. 166–70.
Blaug, M. (1968) *Economics of Education* (London: Penguin).
Blaug, M. (1970) *An Introduction to the Economics of Education* (London: Allen Lane).
Bliss, C. J. (1975) *Capital Theory and the Distribution of Income* (Amsterdam: North Holland).
Britto, R. (1972) 'On differential savings propensities in a two class growth model', *Review of Economic Studies*, Vol. 39, pp. 491–4.
Bruno, M. (1969) 'Fundamental duality theorems in the pure theory of capital and growth', *Review of Economic Studies*, Vol. 36, pp. 39–54.
Bruno, M., Burmeister, E. and Sheshinski, E. (1966) 'The nature and implications of the reswitching of techniques', *Quarterly Journal of Economics*, Vol. 80, pp. 526–53. Also in Newman (1968).

177

Burmeister, E. (1974) 'Synthesising the neo-Austrian and alternative approaches to capital theory: a survey', *Journal of Economic Literature*, Vol. 12, pp. 413–56.

Burmeister, E. and Dobell, R. (1969) 'Disembodied technical change with several factors', *Journal of Economic Theory*, Vol. 1, pp 1–8.

Burmeister, E. and Kuga, K. (1970) 'The factor price frontier, duality and joint production', *Review of Economic Studies*, Vol. 37, pp. 11–20.

Cass, D. and Yaari, M. E. (1967) 'Individual saving, aggregate capital accumulation and efficient growth', in K. Shall (ed.), *Essays on the Theory of Optimal Economic Growth* (Cambridge, Mass.: MIT Press).

Champernowne, D. G. (1953) 'The production function and the theory of capital: a comment', *Review of Economic Studies*, Vol. 21, pp. 112–35. Also in Harcourt and Laing (1971).

Chang, P. P. (1964) 'Rate of profit and income distribution in relation to the rate of economic growth: a comment', *Review of Economic Studies*, Vol. 31, pp. 103–6.

Chang, W. W. (1972) 'A model of economic growth with induced bias in technical progress', *Review of Economic Studies*, Vol. 39, pp. 205–12.

Chiang, A. C. (1973) 'A simple generalisation of the Kaldor–Pasinetti theory of the profit rate and income distribution', *Economica*, Vol. 40, pp. 311–13.

Craven, J. (1973) 'Stability in a two sector model with induced bias', *Economic Journal*, Vol. 83, pp. 858–62.

Craven, J. (1975) 'Capital theory and the process of production', *Economica*, Vol. 42, pp. 283–92.

Craven, J. (1977) 'On the marginal product of capital', *Oxford Economic Papers*, Vol. 29, pp. 472–8.

Craven, J. (1978) 'Technical progress in a multisectoral model', unpublished paper (Canterbury, University of Kent).

Craven, J. (1979) 'Efficiency curves in the theory of capital: a synthesis', in K. E. Schott and K. D. Patterson (eds), *The Measurement of Capital: Theory and Practice* (London: Macmillan).

Debreu, G. (1959) *Theory of Value*, Cowles Foundation Monograph No. 17 (New York: Wiley, for Yale University, New Haven, Conn.).

Desai, M. (1974) *Marxian Economic Theory* (London: Gray Mills).

Diamond, P. A. (1965) 'Technical change and the measurement of capital and output', *Review of Economic Studies*, Vol. 32, pp. 289–98.

Dixit, A. (1976) *The Theory of Equilibrium Growth* (London: Oxford University Press).

Dixit, A. (1977) 'The accumulation of capital theory', *Oxford Economic Papers*, Vol. 29, pp. 1–29.

Dobb, M. (1973) *Theories of Value and Distribution since Adam Smith* (Cambridge: Cambridge University Press).

Eltis, W. A. (1973) *Growth and Distribution* (London: Macmillan).

Ferguson, C. E. (1969) *The Neoclassical Theory of Production and Distribution* (Cambridge: Cambridge University Press).

Ferguson, C. E. (1972) 'The current state of capital theory: a tale of two paradigms', *Southern Economic Journal*, Vol. 39, pp. 160–76.

Findlay, R. (1967) 'Neutral technical progress and the relative stability of two sector growth models', *International Economic Review*, Vol. 8, pp. 109–15.

Fisher, I. (1930) *The Theory of Interest* (New York: Macmillan).

Garegnani, P. (1966) 'Switching of techniques', *Quarterly Journal of Economics*, Vol. 80, pp. 554–67.

Garegnani, P. (1970) 'Heterogeneous capital, the production function and the theory of distribution', *Review of Economic Studies*, Vol. 37, pp. 407–36.

Graaff, J. de V. (1957) *Theoretical Welfare Economics* (Cambridge: Cambridge University Press).

Green, H. A. J. (1971) *Consumer Theory* (London: Penguin).

Hagemann, H. and Kurz, H. D. (1976) 'Reswitching of techniques in neo-Austrian models', *Kyklos*, Vol. 29, pp. 678–708.

Hahn, F. H. (1965) 'On two sector growth models', *Review of Economic Studies*, Vol. 32, pp. 339–46.

Hahn, F. H. (ed.) (1971) *Readings in the Theory of Growth* (London: Macmillan).

Hahn, F. H. and Matthews, R. C. O. (1964) 'The theory of economic growth: a survey', *Economic Journal*, Vol. 74, pp. 779–902. Also in American Economic Association and Royal Economic Society (1965).

Harcourt, G. C. (1969) 'Some Cambridge controversies in the theory of capital', *Journal of Economic Literature*, Vol. 7, pp. 369–405.

Harcourt, G. C. (1972) *Some Cambridge Controversies in the Theory of Capital* (Cambridge: Cambridge University Press).

Harcourt, G. C. (1976) 'The Cambridge controversies: old ways and new horizons – or dead end', *Oxford Economic Papers*, Vol. 28, pp. 25–65.

Harcourt, G. C. and Laing, N. F. (eds) (1971) *Capital and Growth* (London: Penguin).

Harrod, R. (1948) *Towards a Dynamic Economics* (London: Macmillan).

Hicks, J. R. (1932) *The Theory of Wages* (London: Macmillan).

Hicks, J. R. (1965) *Capital and Growth* (London: Oxford University Press).

Hicks, J. R. (1970) 'A neo-Austrian growth theory', *Economic Journal*, Vol. 80, pp. 257–81.

Hicks, J. R. (1973) *Capital, and Time* (London: Oxford University Press).

HMSO (1975) *Royal Commission on the Distribution of Income and Wealth: Report 1*, Cmnd 6171 (July 1975); *Report 2*, Cmnd 6172 (July 1975); *Report 3*, Cmnd 6383 (January 1976) (London: HMSO).

Johnson, H. G. (1973) *The Theory of Income Distribution* (London: Gray Mills)

Jones, H. (1975) *An Introduction to Modern Theories of Economic Growth* (London: Nelson).

Kaldor, N. (1955) 'Alternative theories of distribution', *Review of Economic Studies*, Vol. 23, pp. 83–100. Also in Stiglitz and Uzawa (1969).

Kaldor, N. (1957) 'A model of economic growth', *Economic Journal*, Vol. 67, pp. 591–624.

Kaldor, N. (1960a) 'A rejoinder to Mr Atsumi and Professor Tobin', *Review of Economic Studies*, Vol. 27, pp. 121–3.

Kaldor, N. (1960b) *Essays on Value and Distribution* (London: Duckworth).

Kaldor, N. (1966) 'Marginal productivity and the macroeconomic theories of distribution', *Review of Economic Studies*, Vol. 33, pp. 309–19. Also in Harcourt and Laing (1971).

Kaldor, N. and Mirrlees, J. A. (1962) 'A new model of economic growth', *Review of Economic Studies*, Vol. 29, pp. 174–92. Also in Sen (1970b), Stiglitz and Uzawa (1969) and Hahn (1971).

Kalecki, M. (1954) *Theory of Economic Dynamics* (London: Allen & Unwin).

Kalecki, M. (1971a) *Selected essays on the Dynamics of the Capitalist Economy* (Cambridge: Cambridge University Press).

Kalecki, M. (1971b) 'Class struggle and the distribution of national income', *Kyklos*, Vol. 24, pp. 1–9.

179

Kennedy, C. (1962) 'The character of improvements and of technical progress', *Economic Journal*, Vol. 72, pp. 899−911.

Kennedy, C. (1964) 'Induced bias in innovation and the theory of distribution', *Economic Journal*, Vol. 74, pp. 541−7. Also in Stiglitz and Uzawa (1969).

Kennedy, C. (1966) 'Samuelson on induced innovation', *Review of Economics and Statistics*, Vol. 48, pp. 442−4.

Kennedy, C. (1968) 'Time, interest and the production function', in J. N. Wolfe (ed.), *Value, Capital and Growth: Papers in Honour of Sir John Hicks* (Edinburgh: Edinburgh University Press).

Kennedy, C. (1973) 'A generalisation of the theory of induced bias in technical progress', *Economic Journal*, Vol. 83, pp. 48−57.

Kennedy, C. and Thirlwall, A. P. (1973) 'Technical progress: a survey', *Economic Journal*, Vol. 83, pp. 11−72. Also in Royal Economic Society and Social Science Research Council (1973).

Keynes, J. M. (1936) *The General Theory of Employment, Interest and Money* (London: Macmillan).

King, J. and Regan, P. (1976) *Relative Income Shares* (London: Macmillan).

Knight, F. H. (1921) *Risk, Uncertainty and Profit* (New York: Harper & Row).

Koopmans, T. C. (1957) *Three Essays on the State of Economic Science* (New York: McGraw Hill).

Kregel, J. A. (1976) *Theory of Capital* (London: Macmillan).

Laing, N. F. (1969) 'Two notes on Pasinetti's theorem', *Economic Record*, Vol. 45, pp. 373−85.

Levhari, D. E. (1965) 'A nonsubstitution theorem and switching of techniques', *Quarterly Journal of Economics*, Vol. 79, pp. 98−105.

Levhari, D. E. and Samuelson, P. A. (1966) 'The nonswitching theorem is false', *Quarterly Journal of Economics*, Vol. 80, pp. 518−19.

Malinvaud, E. (1953) 'Capital accumulation and the efficient allocation of resources', in K. J. Arrow and T. Scitovsky (eds), *Readings in Welfare Economics*, (London: Allen & Unwin).

Malinvaud, E. (1961) 'An analogy between atemporal and intertemporal theories of resource allocation', *Review of Economic Studies*, Vol. 28, pp. 143−60. Also in Stiglitz and Uzawa (1969).

Malthus, T. R. (1798) *An Essay on the Principle of Population* (reprinted in 1970, London: Penguin).

Marx, K. (1867) *Capital*, 3 Vols (reprinted in 1974, London: Lawrence & Wishart).

Mayston, D. J. (1974) *The Idea of Social Choice* (London: Macmillan).

McCain, R. A. (1972) 'Induced technical progress and the price of capital goods', *Economic Journal*, Vol. 82, pp. 921−33.

Meade, J. E. (1966a) 'Life cycle savings, inheritance and economic growth', *Review of Economic Studies*, Vol. 33, pp. 61−78.

Meade, J. E. (1966b) 'The outcome of the Pasinetti−process: a note', *Economic Journal*, Vol. 76, pp. 161−5. Also in Harcourt and Laing (1971).

Mincer, J. (1958) 'Investment in human capital and personal income distribution', *Journal of Political Economy*, Vol. 66, pp. 281−302.

Morishima, M. (1966) 'Refutation of the nonswitching theorem', *Quarterly Journal of Economics*, Vol. 80, pp. 520−5.

Morishima, M. (1973) *Marx's Economics: A Dual Theory of Value and Growth* (Cambridge: Cambridge University Press).

Morishima, M. (1974) 'Marx in the light of modern economic theory', *Econometrica*, Vol. 42, pp. 611−32.

Morishima, M. (1976) 'Positive profits with negative surplus value – a comment', *Economic Journal*, Vol. 86, pp. 599–603.

Morishima, M. and Catephores, G. (1978) *Value, Exploitation and Growth* (London: McGraw Hill).

Newman, P. (ed.) (1968) *Readings in Mathematical Economics*, 2 vols (Baltimore: Johns Hopkins Press).

Ng, Y. K. (1974) 'The neoclassical and neo-Marxist Keynesian theories of income distribution', *Australian Economic Papers*, Vol. 13, pp. 124–32.

Nuti, D. M. (1970) 'Capitalism, socialism and steady growth', *Economic Journal*, Vol. 80, pp. 32–54. Also in Harcourt and Laing (1971).

Orosel, G. (1977) 'Capital gains and losses and the existence of a steady state in multisectoral models with induced technological progress', *Economic Journal*, Vol. 87, pp. 315–23.

Oulton, N. (1974) 'The distribution of education and the distribution of income', *Economica*, Vol. 41, pp. 387–402.

Pasinetti, L. L. (1960) 'A mathematical reformulation of the Ricardian system', *Review of Economic Studies*, Vol. 27, pp. 78–98. Also in Newman (1968) and Pasinetti (1974).

Pasinetti, L. L. (1962) 'Rate of profit and income distribution in relation to the rate of economic growth', *Review of Economic Studies*, Vol. 29, pp. 267–79. Also in Sen (1970b), Hahn (1971) and Pasinetti (1974).

Pasinetti, L. L. (1966a) 'Changes in the rate of profit and switches in techniques', *Quarterly Journal of Economics*, Vol. 80, pp. 503–17.

Pasinetti, L. L. (1966b) 'New results in an old framework', *Review of Economic Studies*, Vol. 33, pp. 303–6.

Pasinetti, L. L. (1974) *Growth and Income Distribution: Essays in Economic Theory* (Cambridge: Cambridge University Press).

Pen, J. (1971) *Income Distribution* (London: Penguin).

Phelps, E. S. (1961) 'The golden rule of accumulation: a fable for growthmen', *American Economic Review*, Vol. 51, pp. 638–43. Also in Sen (1970b).

Phelps, E. S. (1973) *Economic Justice* (London: Penguin).

Phelps Brown, E. H. (1968) *Pay and Profits* (Manchester: Manchester University Press).

Phelps Brown, E. H. (1977) *The Inequality of Pay* (London: Oxford University Press).

Quirk, J. and Saposnik, R. (1968) *Introduction to General Equilibrium Theory and Welfare Economics* (New York: McGraw Hill).

Ricardo, D. (1817) *Principles of Political Economy and Taxation* (reprinted in 1970, London: Penguin).

Robinson, J. V. (1953) 'The production function and the theory of capital', *Review of Economic Studies*, Vol. 21, pp. 81–106. Also in Robinson (1965, Vol. 2) and Harcourt and Laing (1971).

Robinson, J. V. (1956) *The Accumulation of Capital* (London: Macmillan).

Robinson, J. V. (1959) 'Accumulation and the production function', *Economic Journal*, Vol. 59, pp. 433–42.

Robinson, J. V. (1962) *Essays in the Theory of Economic Growth* (London: Macmillan).

Robinson, J. V. (1965) *Collected Economic Papers*, Vols 2 and 3 (Oxford: Blackwell).

Robinson, J. V. (1971) 'The measurement of capital: the end of the controversy', *Economic Journal*, Vol. 81, pp. 597–602.

Royal Economic Society and Social Science Research Council (1973) *Surveys of Applied Economics*, Vol. 1 (London: Macmillan).

Salter, W. E. G. (1960) *Productivity and Technical Change* (Cambridge: Cambridge University Press).

Samuelson, P. A. (1947) *Foundations of Economic Analysis* (Cambridge, Mass.: Harvard University Press).

Samuelson, P. A. (1962) 'Parable and realism in capital theory: the surrogate production function', *Review of Economic Studies*, Vol. 39, pp. 193–206. Also in Harcourt and Laing (1971).

Samuelson, P. A. (1965) 'A theory of induced innovation on Kennedy–von Weizsacker lines', *Review of Economics and Statistics*, Vol. 47, pp. 343–56.

Samuelson, P. A. (1966a) 'A summing up', *Quarterly Journal of Economics*, Vol. 80, pp. 568–83. Also in Harcourt and Laing (1971).

Samuelson, P. A. (1966b) *The Collected Scientific Papers of Paul A. Samuelson* (Cambridge, Mass.: MIT Press).

Samuelson, P. A. (1966c) 'Rejoinder: agreements, disagreements, doubts and the case of induced Harrod-neutral technical change', *Review of Economics and Statistics*, Vol. 48, pp. 444–8.

Samuelson, P. A. and Modigliani, F. (1966) 'The Pasinetti paradox in neoclassical and more general models', *Review of Economic Studies*, Vol. 33, pp. 269–302.

Sato, K. (1966) 'The neoclassical theorem and the distribution of income and wealth', *Review of Economic Studies*, Vol. 33, pp. 331–6.

Sato, R. and Beckmann, M.J. (1968) 'Neutral inventions and production functions', *Review of Economic Studies*, Vol. 35, pp. 57–66 and 366.

Schefold, B. (1976) 'Different forms of technical progress', *Economic Journal*, Vol. 86, pp. 806–19.

Sen, A. K. (1963) 'Neoclassical and neo-Keynesian theories of distribution', *Economic Record*, Vol. 39, pp. 53–64.

Sen, A. K. (1970a) *Collective Choice and Social Welfare* (Edinburgh: Oliver & Boyd).

Sen, A. K. (ed.) (1970b) *Growth Economics: Selected Readings* (London: Penguin).

Solow, R. M. (1956a) 'A contribution to the theory of economic growth', *Quarterly Journal of Economics*, Vol. 70, pp. 65–94. Also in Newman (1968), Stiglitz and Uzawa (1969) and Sen (1970b).

Solow, R. M. (1956b) 'The production function and the theory of capital', *Review of Economic Studies*, Vol. 23, pp. 101–8.

Solow, R. M. (1961) 'A note on Uzawa's two sector model of economic growth', *Review of Economic Studies*, Vol. 29, pp. 48–50. Also in Stiglitz and Uzawa (1969), Sen (1970b) and Hahn (1971).

Solow, R. M. (1974) Review of J. R. Hicks's *Capital and Time*, *Economic Journal*, Vol. 84, pp. 189–92.

Spaventa, L. (1970) 'Rate of profit, rate of growth and capital intensity in a simple production model', *Oxford Economic Papers*, Vol. 22, pp. 129–47.

Sraffa, P. (1951) *Introduction to the Works and Correspondence of D. Ricardo* (Cambridge: Cambridge University Press).

Sraffa, P. (1960) *The Production of Commodities by Means of Commodities* (Cambridge: Cambridge University Press).

Steedman, I. (1975) 'Positive profits with negative surplus value', *Economic Journal*, Vol. 85, pp. 114–23.

BIBLIOGRAPHY

Steedman, I. (1976a) 'Positive profits and negative surplus value: a reply', *Economic Journal*, Vol. 86, pp. 604–8.

Steedman, I. (1976b) 'Positive profits with negative surplus value: a reply to Wolfstetter', *Economic Journal*, Vol. 86, pp. 873–6.

Steedman, I. (1977) *Marx after Sraffa* (London: New Left Books).

Stiglitz, J. E. and Uzawa, H. (eds) (1969) *Readings in the Modern Theory of Economic Growth* (Cambridge, Mass.: MIT Press).

Swan, T. W. (1956) 'Economic growth and capital accumulation', *Economic Record*, Vol. 32, pp. 343–61. Also in Newman (1968), Stiglitz and Uzawa (1969) and Harcourt and Laing (1971).

Takayama, A. (1965) 'On a two sector model of economic growth with technological progress', *Review of Economic Studies*, Vol. 32, pp. 251–62.

Tobin, J. (1960) 'Towards a general Kaldorian theory of distribution', *Review of Economic Studies*, Vol. 27, pp. 119–20.

Uzawa, H. (1961) 'On a two sector model of economic growth', *Review of Economic Studies*, Vol. 29, pp. 40–7. Also in Stiglitz and Uzawa (1969) and Hahn (1971).

von Weizsacker, C. C. (1966) 'Tentative notes on a two sector model with induced technical progress', *Review of Economic Studies*, Vol. 33, pp. 245–52. Also in Hahn (1971).

von Weizsacker, C. C. (1973) 'Modern capital theory and the concept of exploitation', *Kyklos*, Vol. 26, pp. 245–81.

Walras, L. (1890) *Elements of Pure Economics* (reprinted in 1954, London: Allen & Unwin).

Wan, H. Y. (1971) *Economic Growth* (New York: Harcourt Brace Jovanovich).

Wicksell, K. (1901) *Lectures on Political Economy*, 2 vols (English translation 1934, London: Routledge & Kegan Paul).

Wolfstetter, E. (1973) 'Surplus labour, synchronised labour costs and Marx's labour theory of value', *Economic Journal*, Vol. 83, pp. 787–809.

Wolfstetter, E. (1976) 'Positive profit with negative surplus value: a comment', *Economic Journal*, Vol. 86, pp. 864–72.

INDEX

INDEX

Printed in the United States
by Baker & Taylor Publisher Services